LET NOT MY COUNTRY DIE

Also by Credo Mutwa
Indaba My Children
Africa Is My Witness

LET NOT MY COUNTRY DIE

CREDO MUTWA

UNITED PUBLISHERS INTERNATIONAL

Published in South Africa by United Publishers
International (Pty) Ltd.

ISBN 0-620-10290-X

First impression 1986
Second impression 1987

Binding and printing by Sigma Press
(Pty) Limited, Pretoria.

Typesetting by Cityset

To the Memory of Mr Phadima Kupa and
Miss Ramatsimela Teka, Burnt to Death
by Activists in Lebowa

Prayer for a Beloved, Dying Country

An Angry Sun, blood-yellowed, glares askance . . .
Through the heaving clouds of black and stinking smoke
The livid flames leap high, like demon-queens gone mad
Dancing to the drums of unrelenting Hate
The Smell of Death smothers the trembling Land
And Rage, far hotter than dark SATAN's fabled Den
Fills the angry Streets, the screaming Alleys and Avenues of Flame!
Reason is dead; now is the Killer's Hour . . .
As Mercy hides her bloodied Face in shame
The Song of the Rifle invades the sleepless Night
And bullets uncounted ravish the shrieking air
Some spend their lust against uncaring walls . . .
Some crash through Glass seeking the Lives beyond
Youths die unshriven, filled with leaden Death
And Weeping mothers curse the Gods in vain
I smell Teargas where Jacarandas bloomed
And see Bloodstains where Children played before
The riotous Stone hums through the dirtied air
To crash 'gainst steel or shatter human bone
The Petrol Bomb, smoke-tailed, arcs through the shouting night
A brief Comet filled with long-pent-up Rage
The Whetted Panga, astream with guiltless Blood
Is brandished high where none dare plead for Calm
And beneath a rock, hurled by Bloodthirsty Men
A Girl dies guiltless of panga-wounds and flames!
God, where are You? LET NOT MY COUNTRY DIE!
I send my voice to You beyond the Stars
I call to You, God of Countless Names
To You, O Mystery of the Feathered Years
Unseen yet seeing, unknown, yet knowing all
O Shapless Shape beyond the Galaxies
O Source Supreme of all the Things that be
Eternal Flame in which the Stars were born
God of my Fathers! LET NOT MY COUNTRY DIE!
Above this roaring tide of Flame and Death
Above the storm of Hatred and Fear
Above the howls of Men turned Beasts I raise my Plea
O NKULUNKULU, LET NOT MY COUNTRY DIE!
Declare Your will and bid Your Light shine forth
To pierce the Tempest and devour the Dark
And let AZANIA to know Peace once again!

Credo Vusamazulu Mutwa
1986

Contents

Preface

My people, I have written this book as a message calling on you to first try and explore the path of peace rather than the way of violence and confrontation many of you appear to have chosen. I have also attempted to show the world what lies behind the violence that is dementing our country at this moment.

There are very few countries upon the vastness of the African continent about which so much has been thought, spoken and written as South Africa. There are very few countries in Africa, if not in the whole world, about which so much that is bizarre, amusing, nonsensical and lurid has been poured out of the newsmedia of both the West and the Communist Bloc than my country; and there are few countries on earth about which so much is known, and has been revealed, and yet so much remains unknown.

South Africa is a mystery within a mystery; she is the great unknown of our troubled times, and although a thousand lies and half truths have been written about her, the hidden truth about my country is a million times more tragic, amazing and yet more beautiful than any fiction can ever be.

Like all countries upon which the shimmering spotlight of world attention has fallen and remained for a number of years, South Africa's name is enough to start a furious argument among thinking people anywhere on the earth . . . some defending her and some bitterly reviling her. She is what we call in Zulu *"indaba egudwini,"* which means, a topic of fierce argument among marijuana smokers gathered around a ceremonial marijauna-pipe.

In writing this book, I have in many cases thrown a small cat among South Africa's many political pigeons . . . a cat thrown from the moderate people in South Africa who are praying for peace and who just want to be left alone.

Credo Vusamazulu Mutwa
1986

1

Racism ... The Great Peril

The world in which we live is cursed by many beliefs, philosophies and creeds; and humankind is held in bondage by many "isms," "ities," and "acies." These philosophies all have one thing in common, this being their insatiable appetite for bloodshed, violence and all manner of strife, and an overwhelming capacity for deceiving millions, deluding continents, and filling graves with millions of needlessly destroyed people.

It seems that man's mind can give birth to no new philosophy, bring to flower no new religion or creed, without afterwards debasing it and using it as a honed sword with which to end his brother's life.

My people the Zulus say man originated from fishes many dim centuries ago, which is why, by tradition, the eating of fish was taboo in lands where Zulus held sway. And I say that if it is indeed true we originated from fishes, then the primitive slime in which those fishes swam still clings to our minds and souls, making us stupid, short-sighted, fanatical and violent. We do things that not only lead to our own destruction but we do things that bring the threat of final annihilation to the very earth that gave us birth.

Like a spider hopelessly entrapped and entangled in its own web, so is humanity entrapped in its beliefs — some of which were born in the minds of men who, were they to be reborn today, would run screaming in pure terror at the sight of what has developed.

1

It is utterly bizarre and indescribably obscene to see modern men — men who have seen their brothers walk on the moon and in the starry void of space, men who have seen the miracle of organ transplants and men who have looked into the fiery hearts of atoms and stars — killing and maiming their brothers and sisters over beliefs and creeds spawned in the minds of half-savages, dead and buried a thousand centuries ago.

If *democracy* was really created for man's freedom, why then have so many millions been murdered and denied freedom in its name? If *communism* was born to make men equal then why have so many millions been given the final equality of death under its banner? Do you have to kill a man to set him free and do you have to enslave him to show him the road to liberty . . . .

Of all the "isms" that afflict the sons and daughters of man, none is more awesome — none more horribly dangerous — than the thing we know as *racism*. Racism is a thing that has been slowly growing from strength to strength in the last half century or so, and this thing is the only force powerful enough to wipe the seed of man off the face of the earth forever.

Listen to me, respected friends, the greatest danger facing mankind on earth these days is racism and it's accompanying ugly little imps named *sectarianism* and *ethnicism*. It is racism (and not communism) that will bring about a world annihilating nuclear war upon the heads of humankind; and it is racism that will unleash the dogs of Armageddon and turn the life giving plains of our planet into dusty, windswept and radioactive deserts.

What really is racism? Racism is the denial, by one human being, of the humanity of a fellow human being. It is the blasphemy against the name and dignity of the Almighty, translated into unnatural deeds, thoughts and words directed at members of a race other than one's own. What is most horrible about this scourge, this foul disease of the human psyche, is that it tends to afflict not the savages of this earth, but rather nations and people who call themselves "civilized."

In my travels throughout Africa and the continents and islands on the globe, in the last thirty years or so, I have found that racism exists everywhere and that it is growing instead of lessening. I have found racism everywhere, and, of all places, even up in the air aboard an aircraft winging its way through the heavens.

Behind the stinking smokescreen communism has raised since

its bloody birth in 1917, is a far greater peril growing like a poisonous tree in almost all countries upon this earth, and racism has been the name of that tree. And I wish to tell you, respected reader, there is overwhelming evidence that every war fought during the sixty-eight years since the end of the First World War, has either been a straight forward race war or has had strong racial overtones.

The First World War was a war between empires — Germany, the British Empire and France. It was, in short, a bloody gentlemen's war fought by crowned kings; and it was, in its first stages at least, marked by acts of chivalry on both sides — both in the air and on the ground.

The Second World War was totally different; it was actually two wars in one. The first part of the Second World War ended with the defeat of Nazi Germany in 1945; but the second is still going on this very day; and men such as Adolf Eichmann[1] and Kurt Waldheim[2] are casualties of this war.

Future historians will recognize the Second World War as having been the first world war in which naked racism played a prominent part. Behind the thunder and the clamour lay another conflict — that of Nazi against Jew.

A deadly war it was whose shots were fired in tunnels under the ghettos of Warsaw and behind concentration camp walls, such as in Dachau, Buchenwald and Auschwitz. A war that claimed well over six million Jews and that left such a strong residue of bitter, enduring hatred that there are men and women alive among Jewish people today for whom this war will never be over until the last Nazi war criminal is hunted down and brought to justice — and even then it will still not be over.

Apart from the Nazi's racially inspired conflict, the Second World War produced another horrendous race conflict, which, at first glance, seemed to be part of the whole of that fearsome global blood-letting. So, one can say that the Second World War was really three wars rolled into one.

The first of these being the war of Germany against the Allies for the domination of Europe and finally the world; the second being the race war of Nazi over Jew, while the third was the state-cum-race-war between the yellow race of Japan and the white race of the United States of America.

The two race wars hidden within the Second World War did not happen by accident, the groundwork had been laid down by many

3

people in different parts of the world years before the actual blood-letting started.

During the period immediately after the end of the First World War, extremely sinister racist trends emerged and began to grow slowly and insidiously throughout the 1920s and the early 1930s in Europe and in the United States of America. These trends became so widespread and so deep-rooted that they brought about the coming of writers of novels, comic books and other periodicals with racist overtones. The first trend was an upsurge of anti-Semitism, which was prevalent in Germany as a result of thousands of Germans blaming the Jewish people for their defeat during the First World War. The second trend was anti-Mongolism, or the belief in the danger of the yellow peril, which was at that time a popular trend among the intelligentsia in countries such as the USA.

In Germany the National Socialist Party of Adolf Hitler saw, in the prevailing anti-Semitic atmosphere among the grassroots-level of the German people, a golden ladder by which they could climb to power, and they exploited it shamelessly and ruthlessly. Scores of books, magazine articles and other works were produced by writers and were widely read by thousands of people — especially the hot headed and impressionable youth — as the Nazis and their followers went out to condition the entire German nation to look upon Jews with blind, unreasoning and genocidal hatred.

In most novels and thrillers written by Germans during this period, the "villain" was usually depicted as a Jew, while the "hero" was a handsome, blond German. As time went on, books and articles began to emerge that were ostensibly of an objective, scholarly nature, and they produced supposedly scientific proof of the superiority of the Aryan race over other races, and the inferiority and threat of the Jews and other Semitic races to the "Herrenvolk."[3]

Thus, such atrocities as the Holocaust, in which millions of Jews died in concentration camps and gas chambers, were planned many years before; and a nation had been brainwashed for the occasion.

A similar thing was taking place in the USA where writers such as Sax Rohmer, the creator of the fictional character "Doctor Fu Manchu" — an exotic Chinese super-villain — made a lot of money by writing books that exploited the current fear of yellow people, evident in the USA.

The most popular comic strip in newspaper comic supplements was *Flash Gordon*. Flash Gordon was a blond Nordic superhero who crossed swords with *Ming the Merciless.* A yellow skinned alien "emperor" on a planet revealingly named "Mongo." There was another comic strip called *Terry and the Pirates* in which another blonde white hero took on Chinese pirates in a hostile oriental seaport.

All these books and comic strips were exploiting white on yellow racism exactly as German periodicals exploited Aryan on Semite racism. The result was the same, namely hideous racial mass-murder.

Was it years of insidious conditioning that caused the American people to so hate and fear the yellow race as to use not one but two hideous atomic bombs upon an already defeated Japan? I can excuse and rationalize the use of one atomic bomb, but I can never, no matter how much I try, reason away the use of two such weapons.

I met with Americans during my sojourn in the USA who tried to convince me that President Harry S Truman had done the correct thing when he authorized the dropping of the atomic bombs; and that by so doing he saved the lives of tens of thousands of American soldiers, who would have been slain had they tried to storm the beaches of Japan.

But when I went with my wife to Japan in May 1985 and saw the hideous exhibits in the great museum at Hiroshima, I began to loathe the men who had made this decision. Only sheer insane race hatred equal to that of the Nazis, could have driven civilized and supposedly Christian people to have employed a weapon as terrible as this upon a nation already tottering on the brink of defeat. Surely Japan could have been blockaded and starved into surrender, anything but what was done in Hiroshima and Nagasaki.

I noticed something ominous while walking through Peace Park in the city of Hiroshima. I noticed the astonishingly large number of young Japanese school children being brought by bus to this green, yet horribly sad, place; and I asked myself: "Are the Japanese people planning revenge on the USA sometime in the future? Are they too doing what the Jews are doing regarding the Holocaust — teaching their little ones never, never to forget?" Only time, only the passing decades, will tell. But this much I do know: *race wars never end until one or both of the contending races perish.*

In the United States I also met, to my great surprise, a young man who bitterly denied the Holocaust ever occurred; that the whole thing was propaganda put out by, what he called, "Zionist conspirators" in order to besmirch the name of the German people. I told

5

this young bigot the Holocaust was a fact of history, that, further more, I had personally seen, some two years after the end of the Second World War, Jewish people who had emigrated to South Africa who bore marks of the Holocaust on their bodies. I had seen a man and a woman who had muscles surgically removed from their arms and legs as part of a hideous medical experiment in a concentration camp. I had met a woman who had been tattooed with the mysterious name "Feldhure"[4] on her chest by the Nazis. This woman lived in a Johannesburg nursing home where I worked as a cook.

Although I have the deepest sympathy for the Japanese and the Jews for what was done to them during the Second World War, I am by no means blind to the ugly skeletons hiding in the cup-boards of both these people. They too have at times displayed racism towards other people.

I found to my great surprise that there exists a native race known as the *Ainu* in Japan. These Ainu people are even closer in language and culture to Africa than the Japanese are themselves. Even the name by which this race refers to itself — Ainu, which means *human beings* — is very similar to the African words *Anu, Wanhu, Watu,* and even *Bantu,* which mean the same. I strongly suspect that these Ainu must be the descendants of one of the ancient sea-faring races of man that travelled around the globe in unbelievably ancient times, spreading their religion, culture and language to the farthest islands and continents on earth.

I deplore the way Japanese ostracize the Ainu and refer to them as "four footed beasts," and I call upon the Japanese to bring the Ainu out of obscurity so their existence may be acknowledged more closely by people from Africa, and elsewhere.

As for the Jews, I bitterly deplore the shabby way in which some hardline Jewish rabbis have treated the Falasha Jews from Ethiopia, and I beg of the Government of Israel to stop this sort of thing at once. Israel has earned the admiration — some of it grudgingly — of many black people in Africa, and she ought to become a light unto the nations in Africa and not to tarnish her image with deeds that appear racist.

After the end of the Second World War, the world saw the com-ing of yet another war with strong racist overtones, namely the Korean War of 1950-1953, which first started as a war between two Mongoloid states — North Korea and South Korea — and which then spread to involve the Chinese and the Americans.

The next big race war after the Korean War was the infamous Vietnam War, a war in which the United States Air Force dropped more bombs on both North Vietnam and South Vietnam than had been dropped throughout the whole of the Second World War. The Vietnam War was characterized by foul atrocities committed upon unarmed civilians by both sides, notably the massacre at My-Lai[5] and others too numerous to record.

In that war, the Americans suddenly found themselves marooned on blazing islands of homicidal violence, no longer able to tell who was friend and who was foe among the teeming Vietnamese peasants. The USA had repeatedly made mistakes that had totally alienated the Vietnamese, who should have been friendly towards the Americans. Thus, the US soldiers found themselves facing deadly enmity on both sides.

The United States was *bound* to lose the war in Vietnam, because there are no winners in a war between races. The Vietnam War had a number of ominous aftermaths, and in this book I only have space to deal with one of them, the "Boat People of Vietnam."

This episode carries a grim lesson for countries such as South Africa. Vietnam was, outward appearances to the contrary, a country that consisted of several different races of yellow people. Of these races there were two, the native Vietnamese and the Chinese, which had for years lived with deadly hatred for each other — a hatred burning in the darkest recesses of their collective minds. The Chinese were the most economically aware and active race in Vietnam, and most of the many highly-educated and very rich people in Saigon were Chinese. The native Vietnamese, however, were for the most part the downtrodden peasant class and they were both bitterly resentful and envious of the Chinese.

So when the war ended, the Vietnamese decided to avenge themselves upon the Chinese by forcing scores of them into leaky boats, often at gunpoint, and sending them out to sea to perish. Some of these people were rescued by passing ships and by concerned groups and organizations from the United States and other countries. A large majority of these unfortunates, however, died unknown deaths upon the uncaring seas and were never heard from again.

Apart from Vietnam there is another country where there are important lessons to be learnt. That country is The Lebanon, a country once known as "the Nation of Bankers," a country that today has been torn apart by factional, religious, racial and ideological strife — exactly as is happening in South Africa. In fact, when I look at Lebanon I see South Africa as she will be in two or three years time, because Lebanon — formerly one of the wealthiest states in the Middle East — illustrates in a most brutal fashion just how easy it is to destroy a multi-ethnic and multi-cultural country; and the same forces at work in Lebanon are already at work in South Africa.

Racial arrogance, religious intolerance and chauvinism, as well as ranting ideological extremism, are everyday occurrences in the Middle East; and do you not see them all on your television screens in South African news broadcasts? Have you seen the bloody after-math of a clash between members of the Azanian People's Organi-zation[6] and members of the United Democratic Front?[7] Have you seen, on your television screen, the horrifying remains of victims of a clash between members of the United Democratic Front and members of Inkatha[8] in the Chesterville Township near Durban? Did you see the disgraceful brawl between the supporters of the South African Government and those of the Afrikaner Weerstands-beweging?[9]

Supposing all those warring factions in South Africa had been armed with guns, rocket launchers and other modern tools of multiple murder, would it not resemble the Lebanon goings-on? When people start taking machetes and axes to each other how far are they from taking up guns against each other?

Sometime ago the supposedly mad dictator of Libya, Colonel Muammar al-Qaddafi[10] urged black soldiers in the armed forces of the United States to mutiny and overthrow the Reagan Admini-stration; and I am sure that there are many among you, respected readers, who laughed at the Libyan's suggestion, calling it insane and impossible. But I want to tell you this, that a major mutiny by black American soldiers is within the scope of the possible be-cause racism of the most rabid kind is rife in the Unites States. I learned this from reliable and honourable, as well as deeply pat-riotic, American black people.

The United States of America really ought to do itself justice and play down its often strident criticism of South Africa, because it too is guilty of the very offences of which it so fiercely criticizes South Africa. I could write volumes about the cruel racist treatment meted out to Negroes and Red Indians in some parts of the United States. I would not write hearsay but things that I saw.

One day my host, myself, and a number of other people paid a visit to the Miwok Reservation[11] far to the north of Los Angeles. While we were performing a peace ceremony near the sweat-lodge[12] of the leading Miwok medicine-men, a group of students from the local university arrived and asked us to hold a prayer ceremony for a friend of theirs — a fellow-student — who was a political activist and who had been arrested while fighting for Red Indian rights.

Oddly enough, these students were not intending to pray for the release of the young activist, but were praying that he be moved from one state to another. They informed us that of the two states, North Dakota and South Dakota, their friend was imprisoned in South Dakota, a state all Red Indians seem to dread. A Red Indian imprisoned in South Dakota never even received the rudiments of justice and might even be mysteriously murdered in prison. This had happened several times to Red Indian political activists and even ordinary criminals in the past few years.

I was utterly shaken. Deaths in detention — in the USA? I just could not believe it until one of the wrinkled elders told me that it was all true.

"Us Injuns ain't not regarded as humans in this here land my friend," growled, the old Paiute.[13] "Them shitheads in Washington treat us like bums; we live like bums and we die like bums, nobody ever caring none."

I was told that Red Indians had the highest suicide rate of the many minority groups in the USA; that they were being decimated by tuberculosis, alcoholism and other diseases; that in some places Indian lands were being stolen exactly as in olden days. I was told all this and much, much more, until I felt the tears of sorrow misting my bespectacled eyes.

I looked around me beyond the rows of Red Indian faces, some pure-blooded and some obviously of mixed parentage; I saw the pine-clad slopes, the deep brooding valleys of Tualumne,[14] and I asked myself: "God, even here there is the evil thing I thought I had left behind many distances away in South Africa; even here is hatred, racism and bitterness. Is there no place to hide from racism in this world, Almighty God?"

God did not answer, having perhaps gone to attend to things of greater importance elsewhere. I wanted to cry out like a bereaved Zulu woman, so deep was the shock and the anguish I felt after learning how badly the Red Indians are treated in some American states.

So, South Africa is not the only place on earth where there is racism. South Africa is no more a police-state than Great Britain, the USA and other western countries; and while it is true that the South African Police have, for years, played an extremely destructive and negative part in the lives of thousands of black people, in enforcing the Influx Control Laws[15] and other discriminatory laws, the ruthless policing of people has not been confined to South Africa alone. It has been part and parcel of a trend spreading throughout the western world.

There is a Zulu saying that: "He who lives in a pool with crocodiles for long enough, soon grows a snout like one of them," and the meaning of this saying is that very often if you live long enough next to an evil person you tend to adopt some of that evil person's traits and habits. The "free" world has shared the same planet with communistic, totalitarian and terrorist nations, such as the Soviet Union, Cuba, Communist China and Libya, for so long that it has, over the years, grown less and less free and more and more like its enemies in character. I know there are those who would try to dispute this, but it is nevertheless true.

There are ugly and oppressive things that people take for granted throughout the West today. These things were unthinkable in the years before, and even just after, the Second World War.

I know that in the USA, the FBI[16] and the CIA[17] keep secret dossiers on tens of thousands of American citizens of all races exactly as South Africa's security police and National Intelligence Service keep dossiers on scores of prominent South African blacks, coloureds, Indians and whites. I also know that in the USA a policeman has the power to demand proof of identity in the form of a social security card or a driver's licence from a suspect exactly as in South Africa. So what the hell is the difference? Why should South Africa be reviled as a police-state when the entire world has over the years become one gigantic police-cell, one huge prison? Show me any man anywhere in the world today who claims that his native country is a free, truly democratic, country and I will show you a drivelling liar.

Freedom has died throughout the world leaving nothing behind but a dimly seen ghost; and the strange prophecies that the white man George Orwell made in his book, *Nineteen Eighty-Four,*[18] have long since come true.

Nowadays, we live in the age of doublespeak, misinformation and disinformation; as well as rampant hypocrisy and cynicism, where foul tyrants and genocidal maniacs, with the blood of millions on their guilty hands, find it politically convenient to point accusing fingers at other nations, shouting "oppressor! oppressor!"; thus drawing the attention of a deluded and credulous world away from themselves.

There are nations in the Americas, nations in Europe and nations in Africa, as well as in Asia that have no right whatsoever to hurl vitriol at South Africa and to sit in judgement over her, for they are one and all guilty of crimes against humanity just as foul as those of which they accuse my country. I shall name India with her shameful caste system, her bride-burnings and her religious massacres. I shall name Australia, the country that was once accessory to one of the foulest murders in human history, when she and Great Britain deliberately tested an atomic bomb on land they knew to be inhabited by bands of wandering Aborigines, causing the deaths from radioactive fallout of large numbers of these time-hazy people. Thus, sodomites, thieves and rapists have no right to sit in judgement over a harlot!

Racism causes people to do shameful things, the consequences of which they refuse to face afterwards and whose memory they try to erase, as if by doing so they could wipe out the record of the great harm they did on the eternal rock of yesterday's tale. Racism can turn a saint into a bloody-handed, rampaging sinner within moments and it can cause you to inflict terrible harm upon fellow human beings without realizing you have done so.

Believe me, you can be a racist of the most vicious kind without once realizing you are and without admitting that you are. The most rabid racists never admit they are racists any more than an impotent Zulu will ever dare admit that he is "Mr Half-Past-Six." I have discovered much to my great surprise that some of the most rabid racists are deeply religious people who use what is written in the Bible and other holy books to justify and rationalize their racism.

I have also found the most hardened racists skulking among the ranks of the white liberal establishment around the world and in South Africa. I know prominent people in the Liberal and Progressive camp who daily spout a lot of hypocritical drivel about "equal opportunities" and "non-racism" in public, but who in private treat their domestic servants like hounds and who see black people as monkeys who should only be paid peanuts.

I say that racism must be outlawed throughout the world because it is a stumbling block in the path of scientific progress and must be treated as such and urgently removed.

Mankind's conquest of space is fifty years behind according to my calculations, because of Adolf Hitler's racist insanity. While Hitler was in power, German rocket technology was unsurpassed anywhere in the world. Instead of using this technology to explore the frontiers of space, the Nazis chose to fritter away their people's vast energies in a senseless war they were bound to lose, bringing death upon themselves and setting human progress back by many decades.

Mankind cannot afford other Hitlers. Racism must be exterminated from the face of the earth, peacefully, scientifically and permanently . . . NOW.

2

The Roots of Racism in South Africa

Long before apartheid was enshrined within the pages of the great statute books of the Republic of South Africa, it already existed as part of the unwritten laws of this country, as well as other countries in Africa under British colonial rule.

What the Afrikaners did was simply to give an Afrikaans name to something that had existed for centuries in many countries under many different names. Apartheid as we know it today really consists of two ugly things, namely class distinction and racial discrimination.

Not so long ago in South Africa, black taxis carried the legend "second class taxi" on their doors, and the failure on the part of the taxi owner to display this was punishable by law — usually a fine. Also, not so long ago, a restaurant catering for blacks was either known as a "native eating house" or a "second class eating house." Some years ago a sex-crazy black man was arrested and brought before a magistrate in Johannesburg for having made advances to a white woman. After the magistrate had handed down a well deserved sentence he went on to degrade himself, and his high calling, by advising the black man that "in future you must keep to people of your own class." I believe now, and I believed then, that all penis-maddened men, who make unwanted advances towards women of any race, ought to be jailed without mercy. But it seemed to me on that day, in the eyes of the magistrate, black women could be molested with impunity because they were low-class human beings!

What exactly is class distinction and where did it originate? There is no particular country on earth that I can point to as having been the cradle of class distinction because this curse afflicted all countries upon the globe from the very dawn of human history. It was in Europe — particularly in England — that class distinction became a fine art.

From the earliest years of the middle ages, people in England were divided into three distinct classes. There was, starting from the bottom up, the peasant class, the middle class and the upper class. The peasant class consisted of people such as labourers, poor farmers and poor craftsmen. The middle class consisted of well-off or fairly well-off people such as clerks, merchants, country squires and landlords. The upper class consisted of knights, lords, barons, dukes, and earls; and it culminated in the royalty at whose head was the sovereign.

The main distinctions between the peasant class — sometimes called the working class — and the other two classes, were education, pedigree and wealth, these being the criteria by which one's class in society was determined. People who belonged to the peasant class were regarded by both the middle and upper classes as little more than subhuman vermin — to be oppressed, exploited, assaulted and raped with impunity. They had less rights in their native land than rabid dogs had, and they were virtual slaves, from cradle to grave, of the knight, lord or earl who was master of life and death over them; and whose battlemented castles cast ominous shadows over their hovels and crofts at certain times of the day.

This weird caste-system caused intense suffering to thousands of English people over the centuries, and it was often the cause of much blood-letting as the downtrodden peasants strove in vain to free themselves from the chains of servitude and degradation. On more than one occasion in England, rebellious peasants came close to toppling the reigning King.

In the closing years of the 14th century, England and other European countries were devastated by the "black death" that destroyed tens of thousands of human-beings. The result of this awesome mass destruction of human life by the plague, was a serious shortage of skilled and unskilled labour in many parts of Europe and England.

Suddenly the great lords in their crenellated castles realized that there were no willing serfs left to till the land, to tend to the livestock and to repair breaches in the castle walls, for all the hewers of wood and bringers of water had died by the score. What was to be done?

During the reign of King Edward III (1327-1377) a law was passed in England known as the Statute of Labourers, which many in high places saw as the perfect solution to the serious shortage of labour that gripped England; and this law bore strange resemblance to South Africa's Influx Control Laws now being repealed.

Under this law all peasants were forbidden, under pain of imprisonment, or worse, from leaving the farms and the districts of their liege lords and going in search of more lucrative employment elsewhere. This cruel and restrictive law caused great misery and anguish among the English peasantry . . . exactly as South Africa's Influx Control Laws for decades caused great hardship and agony to millions of otherwise law abiding black people.

The English peasants, fettered by statutory restriction of movement and burdened by soul crushing taxation, decided to follow Wat Tyler[19] into the scorching flames of rebellion in 1381, and soon many districts in England were ablaze.

Today, as a direct result of laws similar to the Statute of Labourers, many parts of South Africa are aflame, and there has not been real peace in the country since 1976. Who was that Indian wise man who said that if people fail to learn from the mistakes of the past they will recreate that past and all its mistakes again and again.

Victorian era class distinction was the mother of apartheid. During the reign of Queen Victoria, England sported great manor houses with separate entrances, one for the gentry and the other for people who were euphemistically referred to as "tradesmen." These "tradesmen entrances" were usually at the back of the great house at the end of a long lane. Servants slept either in draughty garrets or in small, cramped airless rooms under a flight of stairs inside the great manor house. They were ill-treated and underpaid, and female servants were regarded as the toys of the lord, who was not above seizing one of them, throwing her onto the kitchen table and raping her violently — later chasing her out like an unwanted dog if she became pregnant.

In those wild and wicked days "getting the parlour-maid into trouble" was something that was greeted with hoots of laughter by upper-class young men; they saw no shame in the appalling crime of mating with a woman, getting her pregnant and then abandoning her to her fate. In Victorian times it was quite common for a upper-class or middle class woman to enter a shop, disrobe in a booth in order to try on a dress, contemptuous of, and oblivious to, the many working class people in the shop with her. Later, that same woman would, when she walked home, not move aside and give way to any working class people she saw coming towards her, but she would walk straight at them forcing them to give way to her.

In South Africa I have witnessed and had personal experience of exactly the same thing as arrogant whites came striding right at me and other blacks on the street, sometimes forcing us off the pavement into the gutter.

When the English left the shores of their native island, in the days of Queen Victoria, to emigrate to newly-discovered and conquered lands in Africa and in the East, they took their shameful class distinction with them to the new colonies. Once there, they no longer applied it to each other but rather to people of other races such as Indians and Africans; and the thing once known as class distinction became known as race discrimination, or, to use a euphemism then popular in those days, the "colour bar."

When former mining camps, such as Johannesburg, became cities with streets, brick or stone homes and multi-storey buildings and factories, Victorian class distinction once more reared its ugly head. Many of the great new buildings in the city centre and stately homes on the fringes of the cities and in the "posh" suburbs began to sport "tradesmen's entrances" and "native entrances" at the rear.

Let no one who loves truth and justice forget that it was the English and not the Afrikaners who brought race discrimination to my country's shores; and let no one who respects fair play forget that it was not Doctor DF Malan,[20] nor was it Doctor Hendrik Verwoerd,[21] who forced black people to carry passes in South Africa; but rather it was Sir George Grey[22] way back in 1854 who first saddled our people with this abominable burden.

Also, let no one delude himself or herself into thinking that race discrimination was non-existent in South Africa before the Nationalist Government came to power in 1948.[23] It was and, as I said before, it was known as the colour bar, a word my people the Zulus corrupted to "Khalabhayi," a word which is still to be found in the Zulu vocabulary to this very day.

3

In the Days of the Colour Bar

The colour bar was to be found throughout the length and breadth of British ruled Africa, in the 1920s as well as the 1930s and right up to the fairly recent 1950s and 1960s. In the early days it was not enshrined in any statute book of course, but it was just as ruthlessly and discreetly enforced as if it were, and its effects on its black victims were just as devastating as statutory apartheid.

For example: during the days of British rule in Africa, black youths were forbidden to continue attending school after they had reached puberty, and the lucky few who carried on with their education after reaching this stage in life, were those who had been taken under the wing of friendly missionaries and taken out of Africa to study overseas. It was because of this policy of setting an age limit on black education by the colonial authorities, that when independence finally came to the African colonies, it was found that very few black people had the standard of education to enable them to take over the many administrative jobs being vacated by colonial officers.

Did you also know that in the 1930s any black man who was employed, say, in a mine compound as a clerk could be dismissed immediately from his job if he dared to buy himself a car?

I once knew a young Xhosa man named Mxolisi Khwekhwe who *was* obsessed with a burning urge to uplift himself and better his lot in life. Mxolisi had started work in the mine as a cook and worked in the kitchen with nine other men. After working at this job for some two years he hit on the idea of learning to speak and write English, a language with which he was deeply fascinated. To this end he befriended a retired old black school mistress and persuaded her to give him lessons in his spare time, and he used part of his modest salary to pay for these lessons. Some time later Mxolisi became so fluent in English that he attracted the attention of the mine officials who quickly promoted him to a position of junior clerk, a job he held with distinction.

Secure in his new job, the young Xhosa began to change both in habits and appearance. He became a natty dresser, favouring white trousers, brown-and-white shoes and a blue blazer. He also grew a pointy moustache, which he lovingly caressed with a dab of petroleum jelly each morning, and he would use a razor blade to create a permanent parting in his hair above the left ear. Very soon he began calling himself Maxwell Quaker, assuming habits and mannerisms that he fondly thought were those of a real English gentleman.

At first this odd behaviour amused the white mine officials; but then one day amusement turned to surprise and anger when Mxolisi bought himself a gleaming second-hand Hudson Terraplane sportscar. He was fired on the spot, disappearing from my life a few days later in a cloud of dust for the valleys of the Transkei, with the elderly school mistress, now his wife, sitting next to him in his new car.

Mxolisi was neither the first, nor the last, black man I saw driven from his job for this reason. There were many others both before and after him, and there were many bizarre things that happened to black people in the days of the colour bar.

Listen, here is another true story: At the turn of the century in Natal a young Zulu man named John Langalibalele Dube[24] — who was gifted with a mind many decades ahead of his time — wanted nothing on earth so much as the privilege of helping his fellow black people by all the means at his disposal. He was a brilliant scholar and the darling of missionaries with his refined manners and agile mind. Dube realized at an early age that if he was ever to achieve anything worthwhile for the Zulu people he first had to acquire an education equal to that of any white man, and so be able to deal with whites on equal terms.

After studying for some time in various mission schools and

colleges, Dube realized that because of the colour bar he stood no chance of acquiring the type of education in South Africa he felt he required. So what was he to do? He chewed over this problem for a long time and then one day a fantastic idea came to him like silver mist into the valleys of his mind. He would escape from South Africa somehow and reach the USA, and there acquire the education he needed.

One day he stowed away aboard a freighter bound for the USA and for two days he remained hidden, seasick, scared, cold and miserable, in one of the holds of the great ship. He would have died of thirst or hunger had not a couple of sailors discovered him in the hold. They frogmarched him, more dead than alive, to the captain's cabin. The captain at first did not know what to do with John Dube . . . should he clap him in irons or throw him overboard? Finally it was decided that the young Zulu could be useful aboard the ship and that he would work his passage to the USA as a stoker — feeding shovelfuls of coal to the roaring and ever-hungry furnaces of the great vessel.

"Ye're as ugly an' as black as the very devil, my bhoyo," said the captain to John Dube. "An' by the Virgin Mary, ye're agonna work like him!"

John Dube finally reached the USA, the land of Booker T Washington[25] and other great men, and there, after great suffering under which a lesser man's spirit would have broken, John Dube at last received the type of education that his heart desired. Some years later he returned to South Africa with an impressive list of degrees behind his name and was immediately seized and thrown into prison by Lord H Kitchener[26] as a "dangerous and troublesome native." Released from prison, Dube went on to become one of the brightest black stars of his time in the South African firmament. He founded a great educational institution known as the Ohlange Mission College[27] in Natal, which still exists to this day, and he went on to establish the first Zulu language newspaper in Natal known as the *Ilanga Lase Natal, The Natal Sun,* which still exists, enjoying a wide readership among Zulu speaking people throughout South Africa.

A mild and peaceloving man, John Dube would have been appalled to see the foul atrocities the African National Congress (ANC)[28] is daily committing on black people in the townships; he would have been horrified to see ANC activists burning people to death with petrol-soaked car tyres in township streets.

John Dube was one of the founder-members of the ANC, which was then known as the South African Native National Congress, and the purpose behind the founding of this organization was to resist the colour bar as well as the many laws of a blatantly racist and discriminatory nature heaped upon the black people — first by the British Colonial Office in London and later by the Government of the Union of South Africa, which was widely resisted by black protest in 1910.

Some of the most discriminatory and most offensively racist laws in South Africa were passed while this country was still part of the British Empire. As far back as 1918 black women marched in protest to Bloemfontein in their hundreds, protesting against a proposed extension of the pass laws to black women.

In 1936 hundreds of black people sold their livestock and gave up their life's savings to raise money so that the African National Congress could take the Government of the Union of South Africa to court for its having laid down a notorious law known as The Land Act of 1936,[29] which prohibited black people from buying farms and owning land outside the "native reserves."

When the 1936 Land Act was passed the entire western world was still in the throes of the great depression whose ripple-effects South Africa too was feeling; and in South Africa hundreds of impoverished white farmers were leaving their farms and streaming into the cities in search of jobs, which were hard to come by.

Very often enterprising and far-sighted blacks managed to buy the abandoned farms and run them fairly profitably, and very soon those white farmers who had managed to hold onto their farms found themselves facing stiff black competition when they tried to sell their produce. So the black farmers had to go, and the Land Act was the one effective weapon of ruining them, dispossessing them legally and sending them packing. The black people lost the battle in court and the Land Act became law, and soon there were no more black farmers to threaten white livelihood.

Did you also know that there was a law in 1925 under which all black people of both sexes and all ages were compelled to get into a specially designed dipping tank to be dipped exactly as cattle and sheep are today? This brutal, degrading and bizarre law was enforced particularly in Durban and other parts of Natal, and doctors had asked for its being passed.

The doctors said that all black people were acrawl with all sorts of vermin, such as lice, nits and bugs; and that "since blacks did not have the minds to remove this vermin on their own the law must do so for them." Thus special dipping tanks were built to which black people were herded, forced to strip and dipped. A disinfectant soap known as *Pumula* was dissolved in water in which the people were dipped. The clothes the people wore were passed through a blast of steam in a boiler room before being dumped on a concrete floor for their owners to find and wear — often while still soaking wet. So who says that race discrimination arrived with the Afrikaners. Who says there was no race prejudice prior to 1948!

4

Culture ... No Excuse for Racism

As we have discussed already, apartheid as we know it today really consists of class distinction and racial discrimination; but there are white conservatives who daily froth at the mouth arguing that there is neither racial nor class differentiation in South Africa — only cultural differentiation. These men and women are liars, lying through their false teeth, and what is more, they know it.

Culture forms absolutely no barrier between black and white in this country; and far from it being a cause of division between people, it has rather served to draw people together. It is well known that over the years, millions of black people in South Africa have adopted nearly every aspect of white culture. They wear western dress, eat western food — much to the detriment of their teeth and general health — enjoy western music, including the classics, and use western cosmetics. In many cases blacks have become more fluent in English and Afrikaans — and other European languages — than they are in their native language. I know many black families that have spoken English and Afrikaans among themselves for generations and they have totally forgotten how to speak their original traditional language.

This much is known by many people, but what is little known is that for well over a century there has been a vigorous cultural cross-pollination going on between the black people and the white people in southern Africa, and that just as there are millions of black people who have adopted western culture in almost its entirety, so are there thousands of white people who have assimilated black culture, and who even feel more at home in it than they feel in their native culture.

I like to keep to the sacred Zulu tradition of talking in pictures and I shall do so now: I want you to imagine two great mountains towering over a little valley, and that one of these mountains is formed of limestone while the other is formed of some kind of black rock. One day a huge limestone boulder becomes dislodged from the slope of the white mountain. At exactly the same time a black stone boulder comes thundering down the slope of the other mountain. The two boulders meet in the valley at the foot of the great mountains and crash thunderously and splinteringly into each other before rolling apart and settling some distance away from each other in the long grass.

Now, if you were to examine both these boulders a short time afterwards, you would find that in their cataclysmic collision they not only pitted, chipped and scoured each other, but they also exchanged some of the substance out of which each of them was created. You would then find that the black stone boulder bore broad smears of powdered limestone while the limestone boulder, for its part, bore wide dark streaks of black stone powder upon its surface.

It has been thus, since time immemorial, that when two ancient cultures meet, they collide — very often bloodily, one seeking to obliterate the other — and they end up having mated with each other and modified each other.

When Alexander the Great[30] stormed into Persia bent on slaying Darius[31] and ramming Greek culture down the Persians' bearded throats, he rode in wearing a typical Greek tunic under his equally typical Greek armour; and his bare, tanned legs were sheathed only in bronze greaves and Greek military boots. But, when he roared out of Persia some time later, seeking the far plains and valleys beyond the Indus River, he was no longer recognizable as a Greek, for he was now wearing Persian armour and typical Persian kingly garb, including long silken trousers under that armour. A conquered people's culture very often conquers the conquerors, and this is as true in South Africa today as it was in Persia so many grey centuries ago.

Nowadays in South Africa there are hundreds of white men and women who prefer living in African-styled thatched dwellings instead of in European-styled homes. It is interesting to note that in nearly all of South Africa's great game reserves and other inland resorts the thatched rondavel[32] type hut is the preferred dwelling for visitors to those places.

In South Africa there are white men and women, who in their thousands now speak Zulu, Xhosa, Sotho, Tswana and even Shangane more clearly and fluently than they speak either of the two official languages, namely English and Afrikaans. And thousands of whites prefer traditional African food to European food.

There are also, in South Africa, many white men and women — some of them world famous academics — who have gone through the traditional African rites of initiation as *inyangas*[33] and *sangomas*[34] and who not only throw the *divining bones*[35] as black traditional healers do, but who take part in sangoma festivities and *coming-out*[36] dances in black townships such as Soweto, Thembisa and others. These people have done much, against almost impossible odds, to promote a clear understanding of black religion and culture among the white population in South Africa. That they have not been given the recognition they deserve by South Africa's universities and by the South African Government, speaks volumes against the shameful mule-headedness of the South African scientific establishments.

It is because of this ignorance that South Africa's flag is stained with the blood of hundreds of needlessly destroyed people, and it is because of this "verkrampte"[37] attitude the shamefully wide communication gap between black and white in South Africa has over the last few years grown dangerously wider.

I used to go on archeological expeditions with the late Mr Adrian Boshier[38] and his wife Joan. Mr Boshier, who was the subject of author Dr Lyall Watson's[39] book on Africa, *Lightning Bird,* was a fully initiated inyanga of the *Moroga*[40] class, a class immediately below the highest class, the *Sanusi*[41] — to which I belong. Last year, 1985, my wife and I travelled to Japan in the company of Professor Len Holdstock, who is not only a psychiatrist of note, but also a qualified sangoma of the Mundawu or Lion class[42] and who is deeply respected by many Soweto sangomas.

But that is not all: In the Johannesburg City Council there is a woman councillor who is a fully fledged sangoma initiated in

Venda, and who has done valuable work in combating hunger and malnutrition in rural and urban areas.

I also happen to know Johnny Clegg, a young white man who is more Zulu than a Zulu and who was co-founder of the famous Juluka dance group that specialized in traditional Zulu music, and which sold thousands of records world wide. I have known Johnny Clegg since he was a lad of about thirteen or fourteen-years-old, when he used to risk arrest by the Johannesburg Municipal Police by disguising himself as a black man in order to gain entry into the Wemmer Black Men's Hostel outside Johannesburg, to play the guitar with his great friend, Sipho Mchunu who was also a founder member of Juluka.

In the few short years he has been on this earth, Johnny Clegg has done much to create goodwill between white and black in South Africa. He and others like him could save South Africa from the holocaust that looms like a dark cloud over its horizon, if only politicians and other self-seekers would get out of the way.

Since the birth of South Africa as a nation, *culture* has played a reconciliatory and not a divisive role in this land. Men such as John Dunn,[43] who became a Zulu chief in the 1870s, Nathaniel Isaacs[44] and the handsome and arrogant Lieutenant Henry Ogle,[45] who married King Shaka's beautiful sister Nomcoba, did not turn their backs upon their English way of life simply because they desired Zulu maidens. No, they were first and foremost attracted and captivated by the proud warrior culture of the Zulu people, finding it deeper and far richer than the fast degenerating English culture.

Even men of the cloth such as Bishop JW Colenso[46] found reason to respect the culture of the Zulus and he came closer to understanding the mysteries of the black man's religion and the finer nuances of the black man's philosophies than any other white person.

To argue that it is culture that divides black and white in South Africa is to indulge in gross deception and furthermore this sort of argument is puerile and fallacious.

5

Roots of Apartheid

The English brought crude race prejudice — based upon supposedly scientific "proof" of the superiority of the caucasian race over other races of man upon this planet — to the shores of this land of ours. The 19th century saw much more than just the Industrial Revolution and the establishment of great empires in the East, in Africa and other parts of the globe by aggressive and ambitious European nations such as Great Britain, Germany, France, Spain, Belgium and Portugal.

The 19th century saw much more than the world-shaking and history changing inventions of men such as Robert Stevenson,[47] Sir Isambard Brunel,[48] Joseph Lister,[49] Alfred Nobel,[50] Rudolf Diesel[51] and Karl Benz,[52] to name but a few of the great men whose achievements still affect our daily lives. It also saw the writings and theories of men whose graves ought to be spat upon, men who, by the outpourings of their diseased and warped minds, were destined to bring death and misery to millions of people as yet unborn for many, many decades; and among these men I count Karl Marx,[53] Charles Kingsley,[54] TE Lawrence[55] and Joseph Smith,[56] founder of the Mormon Church.

These men preached racism. They preached that dark-skinned people were subhuman and that the only the race fit to be called truly human was the white race. Kingsley and Lawrence openly referred to black people as the "lower races" while Smith states in his "Book of Mormon" that certain groups of people "were cursed with dark skins" for breaking some of the laws of God.

Thousands of impressionable young men and women from all over 19th century Europe were slowly poisoned spiritually and mentally by the preachings of these men and others like them, and when the time came for these young people to leave the shores of their native countries for Africa, they were already conditioned to look upon the black people they were to meet there as things less than human at worst, and at best, as lost, sinful people — descendants of Cain or of Ham — who had to be brought back to the path of salvation at all costs . . . by force if necessary.

It was this attitude that drove men like Robert Moffat,[57] David Livingstone[58] and George Stechmann[59] into the depths of Africa. There was nothing else that forced them to endure the hunger, the fever and exposure, the wild animals and the hostile tribes as they ventured deeper and deeper into the very bowels of the continent. Love had nothing to do with it, only a raging desire to play "God on Earth" — a desire that made them totally blind to certain very important truths about the people they believed were only superstition-ridden savages; Godless heathens in urgent need of "salvation." Not once did these missionaries ask themselves exactly why these "savages" were so ready to listen to their sermons and why these "heathens" often went out of their way to shield the missionaries from harm.

It is a fact of history that on the day when the Zulu King Dingane ordered his warriors to kill the Voortrekker leader Piet Retief[60] and his men, the killings were witnessed by a missionary named Reverend Francis Owen[61] who had been allowed by the Zulu King a few years before to open a mission station within sight of the great Zulu kraal. Dingane never once threatened to harm Owen and it was the missionary himself who lost his nerve and fled from Zululand after Retief's death. It is recorded that Dingane was deeply puzzled and hurt by the flight of his white friend "Moaweni."

In the Americas, the Emperor Montezuma II[62] mistook the invading Spaniard, Conquistador Hernando Cortez[63] for the Sun-God, because Cortez had the symbol of the Cross of Montezuma, the sign of the Sun-God, painted on the sails of his ships.

The black people, like the American Indians, believe in a Holy Trinity. They believe in a Son of God and they had laws identical to the Mosaic Code.[64] This and much more helped them to understand the message of Christianity where people of other races in the Orient had failed to understand it and had resoundingly rejected it. It is the uttermost fiction for people to say that any person was ever made to suffer by the black people in the last century as a result of either propagating or having adopted the Christian religion.

The only people who were murdered because they were Christians were the "Martyrs of Uganda" and Bishop James Hannington.[65] They were killed on orders of King Mwanga[66] of the Baganda; and the reason behind these murders was that a violent power-struggle had broken out in central Africa between Christian missionaries on the one hand and Muslim missionaries on the other. The Muslims wanted to extend the Word of Islam into the heart of Africa and they manipulated King Mwanga to reject the Christian missionaries and slaughter black converts to this religion.

In spite of the hideous wars between the Zulus and the Voortrekkers and later the British, my people the Zulus found the time and the inclination not only to listen to the missionaries but to shelter and protect those missionaries from being accidentally killed by the warriors.

Believe it or believe it not, there was a time in South Africa when race prejudice was unknown in many places; when black people, coloureds, Asians and whites lived peacefully side by side on farms and in small villages and towns — too preoccupied with the simple task of keeping the wolf of hunger away from their doors to bother about each other.

Ironically enough, this time of racial peace and tolerance was during the years of the South African republics of the Transvaal and the Orange Free State — now two of the four provinces of South Africa — and in the years that President Paul Kruger[67] held sway in the Transvaal.

In the course of my many years of long research into the past of my country, I have spoken to many very old people in different parts of southern Africa, and they all tell me the same thing. These grey and wrinkled-shrouded men and women of different races tell me that race prejudice only came to South Africa after the Anglo-Boer War of 1899 to 1902.[68]

One very old Griqua[69] woman named Katrina Stoffels told me, years ago, that when she was a girl of fifteen, her father, Jantjie Leeuw, had come across four families of white people who had lost their way while trying to make their way overland by ox-wagon and blundered into a small valley. They were on their way to the Kimberley Diamond Fields[70] "many, many day's journey away," and they had already lost many of their trek-oxen through the depradations of wild animals and through a band of marauding Xhosa cattle thieves that had attacked the caravan two nights before. The families were desperately short of food and water.

Jantjie, who was a minor headman in a small village, went home to fetch some of his own oxen and, assisted by his men, inspanned the beasts to the white people's wagons and pulled them out of the valley to the safety of the Griqua village. Jantjie then ordered his people to give the white travellers all the assistance they required, and for almost a month they stayed with the Griquas.

During the stay, Katrina assisted the white women in preparing food; she was fascinated by the different ways in which they prepared eggs, and by the way they baked bread using the three-legged "Dutch oven" iron pots.

"They taught me how to grind wheat into flour and bake bread in the pot," said old Katrina, "and when I married, I became my husband's favourite wife because I used to bake him bread just as the wit-nooiens (white women) had taught me." And Katrina went on to say that when the white people finally left the Griqua village they left behind little graves — two of their children had sickened and died during the stay.

Throughout this period in South African history before race prejudice appeared, the story is one of shared joys and shared sorrows as the story of Advocate Okert J Bekker[71] shows vividly.

Okert was born just as the Anglo-Boer War was grinding bloodily to a close. The British soldiers were facing determined resistance from "bitter-einder"[72] commandoes under General CR De Wet,[73] who was making such a nuisance of himself that the British now devised ways of dealing with him — extremely unusual ways that were to leave a mark of red bitterness in the hearts of many Afrikaner people.

The British soldiers were not only building chains of blockhouses and other fortifications throughout Natal, the Transvaal and Orange Free State to make things as hard as possible for General De Wet; but they had also begun the rather un-British strategy of burning down Afrikaner farms and carting off hundreds of Afrikaner women and children to concentration camps scattered all over the country. And the purpose of all this was to deny food, sympathy and shelter to General De Wet and his guerrillas. In short the British began to adopt a "scorched-earth" policy.

Now, Okert Bekker's mother had a faithful Basutho servant named Sabina who, when she got wind that the "rooinekke"[74] were coming to burn down the farmhouse and intern her mistress, advised her employer to flee.

"But where shall we go to," asked the distraught white woman, "the rooinekke are everywhere, Sabina."

"We shall go where the red-necks dare not follow us," replied Sabina calmly. "We shall go to Basutholand (Lesotho), Nonna, to the land of my people."

And so the two women escaped from the farm in the dead of the night, carrying what little food and belongings they could. Sabina was leading the way, carrying little Okert Bekker on her back African style, with Mrs Bekker bringing up the rear. In the course of their long and footsore flight, the two women came within an ace of being captured by marauding British patrols, but they finally reached Maseru safely. It was here that little Okert, one day to become a prominent newspaperman and advocate, was brought up like a Basutho child — being fed milk and putu[75] by hand by Sabina and being given an enema with a short length of reed when sick.

Then things changed I am told. The first signs of apartheid began to appear in South Africa with the formation of Afrikaner political parties and groups such as the Broederbond[76] — a highly secret society — and the Ossewa-Brandwag,[77] which was an extremely militant racist organization, that, together with the Broederbond, was fighting to unite the deeply divided Afrikaner people. They fought to instill pride and courage as well as a cold determination into the failing and downtrodden hearts of the Afrikaners, with the view of creating, at some future date, a grand new Afrikaner state out of the then Union of South Africa.

Please make no mistake, the Afrikaners of that period were the cringing serfs while the British were the domineering overloads. Afrikaners found themselves in exactly the same position the blacks find themselves in today. They were a defeated, demoralized nation, having lost not only freedom but unity and dignity after the Anglo-Boer war and other minor conflicts that followed such as the 1914 Rebellion[78] and the 1922 General Strike.[79]

Poverty-haunted and hamstrung by a lack of education, the Afrikaner of those years was an object of ridicule in the eyes of other people in South Africa. He could not fit into the pre-war industrial world, knowing only how to till the land, grow crops and raise livestock. His culture and his language were despised by the British, and I know that some mission-schools in Natal bitterly discouraged black children from learning the "boer" language. Some Afrikaners were even forced to change their surnames; they adopted English surnames and an English way of life in order to find headway in the hostile environment of that time.

I do not know exactly when the incredible secret organization known as the Broederbond was formed, by whom and exactly where, but I do know it worked hard at planning the future of the Afrikaner people, at reviving and revitalizing the colourful Afrikaans language and culture, and readying the Afrikaner people for the role that they were to play in a future Afrikaner dominated South Africa.

In order to unite the Afrikaner people within the shortest possible time, these organizations began to move more and more into extremely dangerous ground . . . they began to exploit racism in its most abhorrent forms in order to fill each wavering Afrikaner's heart with a nameless dread as well as an all-consuming anger.

Again, and yet again, the minds of the Afrikaner people were assailed with the idea that they were God's chosen people who, although destined to rule South Africa, were at present facing a threat of enslavement and extinction at the hands of three barbaric and Godless races — Jews, English and Blacks. And that only by coming together and standing shoulder to shoulder within the bristling spiritual "laager"[80] that the Broederbond was building for them, could "die Boere" hope to overcome this threat.

The large festering wounds of the past in the soul of Afrikanerdom were deliberately opened and deepened with skillfully written pamphlets, newspaper articles, cartoons and blazing oratory; and it was not long before the Afrikaners were welded into one boiling, angry mass, shouting to the highest heavens for freedom and dignity.

Long ignored historical events such as *The Great Trek,*[81] *The Murder of Piet Retief*[82] and the *Battle of Blood River*[83] were brought down from the dusty attics of oblivion; dusted, polished and given a new significance and relevance by the new breed of rabble-rousers the Afrikaner nation had produced. These rabble-rousers let no opportunity go by in which they did not play with Afrikaner emotions as a skilled troubadour of old used to play with the strings of his harp.

Oh, I remember well the blistering Afrikaans language newspaper articles of those years. I remember well the cartoons of those times, usually by a man named Boonzaire who loved to portray capitalism as a grossly fat mustachioed freak he called *Hoggenheimer.* I also remember a poster called *"Die Basterplakkaat."* which appeared in large numbers at election time. It was a poster that warned against inter-racial sex or marriage and it portrayed black men as monsters who had a secret craving for white women and who sought to swamp the Afrikaner by sheer weight of numbers and to absorb him as a people.

In those fierce and eventful days that marked the rise of the Afrikaner people as a nation and as a formidable political force, there were Afrikaner politicians as well as religious leaders who did, said and wrote short-sighted, irresponsible and even frankly terrible things on many unforgotten occasions. They did and said things that had the cumulative effect of kindling and entrenching a bitter enmity in the hearts of black people, especially for the Afrikaner and all he stands for in South Africa.

Again and again in Parliament at election rallies, and even on solemn occasions such as gatherings at the Voortrekker Monument[84] in celebration of important occurrences in Afrikaner history, Afrikaner politicians let no opportunity go by in which they did not stress, and stress again, the point that the black man was an enemy and a threat to the Afrikaners' existence. The black man had to be kept firmly in his place.

The day once known as *Dingaan's Day* and now known as the *Day of the Vow* — December 16 — which recalled a great Afrikaner victory over the forces of the Zulu king, Dingane — which should have been celebrated with dignity, with peaceful music and ringing joy — over the years became defiled by extremely inflammatory speeches, by tooth gnashing rage and crowd hysteria, as well as by deeds of a most violent nature done to black people.

It is known to many blacks of my age group that in the 1930s as well as the early 40s on farms throughout the Orange Free State, the Transvaal and Natal — especially in Natal — black people living and working on white-owned farms took to the bush and hid on *Dingaan's Day* for fear of being assaulted by their employers.

During these times any well-dressed black man who dared show his face in the streets of certain small towns in the Transvaal, Orange

Free State and even the Cape was immediately set upon and beaten up by Afrikaners who accused him of trying to impress their womenfolk and of making a "wit mens"[85] out of himself.

We were dressed to kill on that memorable day in 1938, my friend Ezrom Dhlamini and I. We were on our way from Johannesburg to the small town of Standerton, in the eastern part of the southern Transvaal, to attend the wedding of Ezrom's youngest sister. Ezrom was wearing a grey suit, black shoes and an American-style fedora, and he carried a briefcase and a walking stick. I was wearing a dark blue serge suit, a white shirt and a black bowtie. My feet were encased in brown golf-shoes, and a straw boater with a red and dark blue band around it sat shadily upon my head. In my right hand I swung a furled black umbrella.

We were feeling as bold as a thousand lions when we got off the train at Standerton Station on that cool and cloudless day. Black men stared enviously at us and black girls followed us with their doe-like eyes, sometimes tittering shyly with their hands over their mouths. Our chests swelled with arrogance and pride that we, the bright boys from Johannesburg, were showing these small-town yokels a thing or two about dressing well. Ezrom kept on producing a small mirror out of his pocket and admiring himself in it time and time again; and he was doing just that when we turned a corner and entered the town's main street. Then . . .

"Verdomde kaffirs! Kom hierso, julle! — dumb kaffirs! come here!"

The harsh Afrikaans command froze the very marrow in my bones and for several seconds I was paralysed with terror. Ezrom whirled around, his mouth falling open and his eyes bulging like those of a strangled carp. Then he yelled: "Baleka Mutwa, Safa — run away Mutwa, we are about to die today."

We tried to run but our assailants outran us, and for the next twenty minutes, things were howlingly painful as six white men surrounded and taught us the South African facts of life . . . with fists, sjamboks[86] and thick leather belts.

It is written in the stars that no man on earth can escape his fate, and one thing Ezrom Dhlamini and I were not destined to escape, was the good beating we got on that bright December day. And it was then that I became aware of an interesting thing, namely, that fat people ought to thank God for the thick layers of blubber that He has padded their bodies with — because when you are fat, fists and sticks can warm up your hide, but can rarely break your bones. After that great thrashing I thanked God, and all my shadowy ancestors, that I had been born fat. Ezrom was not so fortunate because he emerged from that hell with a broken arm and a sprained ankle.

I do not know when our assailants decided to call it a day and cease beating the stuffing out of us, but cease they did and their leader — one of the tallest Afrikaners I had ever had the doubtful honour to meet — snarled at us:

"Kaffirs! Swarteterte! Bliksems! Staan julle op! — Kaffirs, stand up!"

We tottered to our feet and were then ordered to take off our suits, shirts and shoes, and leave them on the ground. When we had done that we were told, in no uncertain terms, to get the devil out of Standerton if we did not want to be "dondered"[87] again. We quickly departed, clad in our "long Johns" and socks, our bodies on fire with pain and our nostrils streaming with blood.

Some hours later we reached the house of Ezrom's uncle where the wedding was taking place. Ezrom's relatives took one look at us and immediately inspanned two donkeys to a small green cart and hurried us to the surgery of the local Indian doctor. The doctor worked long and hard with iodine, cotton-wool and bandages to repair our injuries. He pointed out to us a fact we had fatally overlooked: that we had been asking for trouble by showing ourselves well-dressed in Standerton on that particular day.

"Today is Dingaans Day, December 16," said the doctor sadly, "and gangs of young boers in this town never fail to injure or even to kill some of you blacks on this day. So next time you wish to do something stupid such as visiting Standerton on Dingaan's Day, you must first make your wills, kiss your wives and children goodbye, and then pray to Allah and the Prophet Mohammed to grant your souls safe entry to Paradise. Do I make myself clear, gentlemen?"

6

The Poker that Stoked the Flames

For nearly four decades now, since the days of the colour bar, the black people of South Africa have been ruled with a rod of iron. For all these years the black people have been horribly repressed; having being denied the legitimate channels of protest and of airing their grievances. For all these years the black man has endured all . . . while boiling rage built up within him like a volcano about to explode.

In the streets of cities such as Johannesburg, it was a very common sight, in the 1950s, to see long strings of black men, all joined together by handcuffs, marched off to prison after pass offence arrests.[88] When whites saw such sorry sights, sights of as many as sixty arrested blacks being taken away, they rejoiced in their hearts because South Africa now had a strong government that was putting the black firmly in his place, and making South Africa safe for white civilization.

It comes as no surprise to me that townships such as Diepkloof, Meadowlands, Thembisa and Alexandra have nowadays become screaming, stinking and flame-crowned hell-holes of rioting, multiple murders and all sorts of anarchy, because in the 1950s and 1960s all these townships were the most brutally policed black "locations"[89] in South Africa.

In these townships pre-dawn raids for visiting permits were a fact of life to thousands of terrorized residents and they were mounted almost daily by gangs of the infamous *"Black Jacks"* — black Johannesburg policemen characterized by black uniforms, black boots and peaked caps. The Black Jacks were an ill-trained, ill-disciplined horde of hooligans with an almost insane hatred for township householders. These men, many of whom could neither read nor write, were almost all migrant labourers from Transkei, Venda, Gazankulu, and even Lesotho. They were embittered men who had left their families far behind them and who therefore saw fit to vent their blistering choler upon the settled township residents who lived with their families in rows of "matchbox" houses that constitute the townships.

During these permit raids people were often brutally beaten-up by these thugs. You could get a fist right between the eyes from one of these dogs if you were late in opening your door when a Black Jack pounded upon it with his knobkierie.[90] When the Black Jacks entered your home they behaved like demons unleashed; and as townships homes are often overcrowded — with some of the people sleeping on the floors of the various rooms — they would rip blankets off the many sleeping forms . . . some of them naked in the heat of the African night, shine torches into startled faces and shout, "Pass! Permit! Come on, hurry up!"

The poor souls who did not have the required documents were ordered to dress quickly, then shoved out of the house into a waiting "kwela-kwela"[91] van in the street outside, sometimes without shoes, hats or scarves.

The Black Jacks were shamelessly corrupt. If they found a visitor in your home whose visiting permit was, say, three days from expiry, they would tear the permit up and threaten to arrest the visitor unless he or she paid them ten or twenty rand, and most householders chose to pay this money rather than see a beloved relative or friend being dragged off to prison. During permit raids, a person whose papers were in order still risked arrest if found in the wrong house — a house other than the one in which he or she was registered as staying.

A lusty, middle-aged friend and neighbour of mine named Paulus was unfortunate in that he was married to a huge, fat and soaking drunkard of a wife. One day he fell in love with a young widow who had lost her husband some three years before and who lived in a house opposite his across the dusty street. Paulus developed a dangerous habit of creeping out of his house at dead of night and going over to the busty young widow's house to enjoy her hot embraces, while his stinking wife snored the hours away on her old and creaky bed.

Then one night, just as he was drifting off to sleep after a hectic session with his lover he heard the loud barking of dogs in the night and fierce pounding of steel township doors. He jumped off the bed, snatched his trousers from the chair onto which he had flung them some three hours before, pulled them on and made for the bedroom window. Then a savage pounding reverberated through the darkened rooms of the widow's house.

"Open this door immediately! Police!," roared a voice. My friend threw the window open and literally hurled himself out to fall on hands and knees in a small flowerbed immediately below the bedroom window. Before he could get up and run for dear life, a sjambok caught him across his back in a savage blow that tore a scream out of his throat.

He heard an ugly voice say: "Stay right where you are, you stupid bastard! permit!"

Paulus was arrested together with many others and taken to the security superintendent's office where he paid an admission-of-guilt fine for not carrying his pass and was released late in the afternoon. When he returned home his wife went for him the moment he showed his face at the door, her face like a wide-nostrilled and red-eyed rhinoceros. She broke a broomstick across his skull and buried a fist in his stomach, before he managed to escape and seek sanctuary in my house for some hours until my wife and I had succeeded in calming the infuriated woman.

In Alexandra township permit raids were mounted not only in the small hours of every morning, but also right through the day as well. A woman could be arrested while getting water from a tap less than seven metres away from her house.

I recall one particularly repulsive incident in Alexandra when a pregnant woman was arrested while making her way to the local clinic, and while she was sitting on a bench together with other arrested people in the offices of the Peri-Urban Board,[92] her labour pains began, and instead of calling an ambulance the brutal men in that office ordered her to "get out . . ."

Black men who were arrested under the pass laws in the centre of Johannesburg and in places such as Alexandra Township often disappeared for months without trace, having been sold as prison labour to potato farmers in Bethal many kilometres from Johannesburg. Some of these men never returned home alive; they were murdered — beaten to death — by some of the white farmers in this small farming town.

This was South Africa under Prime Ministers such as Dr DF Malan, Mr Johannes Strijdom[93] and Dr Hendrik Verwoerd. A cold brutal country ruled by overconfident men who did not realize their shortsighted actions were planting the seeds of future disaster for all of us. Today we are suffering as a direct result of these men's shortsightedness and arrogance. Today I watch with horror as the minds of thousands of my people, rotted by decades of pent-up rage and hate, drive them into doing deeds for which the very stars hang their bright heads in shame.

7

He Who Sows Burning Coals Will Reap Flames at Harvest Time

So goes a Basutho proverb, and its meaning ought to be clear to all. Exactly what is the truth behind the violence that we see in South Africa nowadays? Is it because of "heightened black expectations" flowing from the present reform initiatives of the South African Government?

This statement, so dear to the South African Government, is absolute puerile nonsense — logical though it may seem to European minds. The flame-edged violence we see in South Africa, on television sets all over the world, has far deeper roots than most people think. It is more than mere political protest of an extremely destructive kind. It is rather one of the many manifestations of storms of agony that howl through the gorges and valleys of the mind of every black man, woman and child alive in this country today.

Today there are dark thunder clouds gathering above the horizon of my native land whichever way I look. In the sunset years of my long earthy life, I see my country, South Africa, facing a threat so monstrous, so utterly terrible, that I sometimes wish I could change myself into a hare and hide in the deepest and darkest hole I can find in the African bush.

What South Africa faces nowadays, is no ordinary revolutionary terrorist war, but a devastating race war of the type that neither side can win, a war that would drag on for years and decades and plunge South Africa into a new dark age, out of which she would not be able to emerge for the next fifty years . . . if ever. A war that would sweep away tens of thousands, aye, even millions, of precious human lives and leave nothing but heaps of rubble where great cities stood before, and blackened acres and bleached animal skeletons where great farms flourished.

And the aftermath of that hideous blood-letting would be a shattered and irreparable economy, mass starvation and disease on a unprecedented scale; and yet more conflict and genocide as different black factions struggle for non-existent power among the ruins of a land wrecked beyond all hope of recovery.

We owe this darkly threatening disaster, this looming tragedy on an unheard of scale, to blundering incompetence on the part of the various (Nationalist) governments in dealing with black restlessness and protest in the course of the last thirty years or so. We owe it to blindness, unreasonableness and inflexibility on the part of the Government on the one hand and to cold, cunning, ruthlessness and double-talking standards on the part of black leaders and agitators on the other, and I will be coming to this in a later chapter.

One of the causes of black anger is words that were uttered by Dr Verwoerd to the effect that there were certain educational heights that the black man could not be allowed to reach, and that he must be given only that type of education that would enable him to fulfill a merely subservient role in South Africa.

Those words were uttered almost thirty years ago when the South African Government established a system of education specially for black children known as "Bantu Education."[94] They were uttered by a man whom the dark mists of death have long since claimed; but they are still as hurtful and as humiliating today to thousands of young black men and women as they were on the day they were first uttered. What is more, they have been used again and yet again by self-seeking black demagogues and left-inclined white trouble makers to effectively feed the roaring furnaces of rage and frustration in the hearts of black youths who were not even born on the day Verwoerd spoke them.

Yes, there is much truth and wisdom in the Barotse[95] saying that: "The human mouth cannot plough a cornfield, nor can it hollow out a canoe or weave a fish trap, but it can cause the destruction of whole tribes."

Like all warrior people who still live close to the earth the

Afrikaner (not all Afrikaners) believes in authority, discipline and obedience. To him black is black and white is white and there are no shades in between, and to him people must either show absolute obedience to authority or suffer. A length of wood must either bend or break; it must "buig of bars" goes the saying in Afrikaans. This rather dangerous mental attitude of "obey or else" has been the driving force behind the Government's method of dealing with black people for many years.

When the South African Government created separate development[96] for the different races in this country, they saw it as the panacea for all ills, the solution to all problems in South Africa — especially to the problem of co-existence between blacks and whites. That this policy was unworkable and would eventually collapse under the weight of its own impracticality, was something that never once occurred to Malan, Strijdom or Verwoerd. To them the solution to the long standing "native problem" was a simple one: separate residential areas, separate amenities and separate homelands. If there were troublemaking malcontents among the blacks, well, the solution *too* was very simple . . . throw them into jail or shoot them.

These Afrikaner leaders refused to accept that separate development was not the cure-all they fondly believed it to be, and that black people had problems and grievances that apartheid could not solve, and that very often apartheid itself, the much touted cure-all, caused even more problems than it solved and more grievances than it assuaged.

A number of extremely strict laws were laid down to combat restlessness and dissent among blacks, Indians, coloured and whites . . . laws the Government found itself being forced to amend and make tougher again and yet again when it found them — much to its surprise — no longer able to have the desired effect. The Government would amend law after law when it learned that — far from lessenning discontent — restlessness and outright subversion were actually increasing in South Africa with each decade the Nationalist Government remained in power.

There are tragic things that have happened in South Africa in the last twenty years or so that have sown the seeds of anger and for which the world has never been given a true explanation. Take for example the tragic accident at Sharpeville on March 21, 1960. That tragedy was brought about as a result of the South African

Government's (with Verwoerd as prime minister) intention to extend the pass laws[97] to black women and this resulted in bitter black opposition.

Do you know *exactly why* black people objected to the extension of these terrible laws to their women folk, and do you, for that matter, know exactly why the groups of black women tried to march on the city of Bloemfontein in 1918?

Let me first tell you this: A large majority of black people do not object to the carrying of identity documents per se; but they did object to the brutal treatment they received at the hands of white and black officials when these documents were being issued to them and when the law itself was enforced.

Incidentally at this very moment, the South African Government, which has just abolished the pass laws, has made known its intention to issue a "uniform" identity document to black, brown and white people alike. If this Government fails to learn from the blood-written books of history — if it refuses to see — that no matter what kind of identity document it issues to blacks, it will be met with bitter opposition if it is accompanied by the racist brutality that used to accompany the issue of "dom-pas" and the enforcing of the laws behind these documents.

When black people applied for a pass-book, they had to wade through the coals of hell itself before they could hold that cursed little book in their hands. Blacks had to go from office to office, stand in queues for days and even weeks on end, spend money on train and bus fares day in and day out and return home empty-handed each evening. By the time the people made any progress they were usually heavily in debt, because of having to borrow money from neighbours and friends to travel to town and stand in queues of misery.

South Africa is cursed with some of the most arrogant and insensitive bureaucrats in the whole world, and so are the national states within her borders. It is very common to see white or black bureaucrats standing about and chatting for hours behind their desks while the silent queues get longer and longer. The former Minister of Bantu Affairs,[98] Dr Piet Koornhof,[99] had faithfully promised our people at one time that these shameful queues would became a thing of the past, but they still exist, hidden away in obscure offices all over the country.

Corruption is rife in some of these offices, especially those in the major centres where the queues are so long that desperate people bribe black queue marshals to take them to the front of the line again and again. It is quite common for a really unscrupulous "queue controller" to pocket as much as thirty or fifty rand in one day.

What I find thoroughly disgusting is that even some of the highest government officials, with whom I have tried to plead, are aware of the situation that daily gives the existing Government a dirty name and which causes enmity in the hearts of thousands of blacks — which no amount of "reform" can wipe out.

This type of corruption was never part of black tradition. If it was, why then did kings such as Shaka[100] and Moshoeshoe[101] punish corrupt indunas[102] by burying them alive or strangling them with strips of hide from the cow they had taken as a bribe? Sometimes a bribe-taking tribal elder had sharp stakes driven into his eyes with a blacksmith's hammer while he was buried up to this neck in sand.

But let me give you an example of the agony a black person had to go through when trying to obtain a reference book, as it was called. I have a daughter, the elder of my two girls, Nozipho, who, on reaching her sixteenth year, was told by her teacher to apply for a reference book.

Nozipho first went to the township manager's office at Diepkloof, Zone Two in Soweto and there, after two days, obtained a letter stating that she was a bona-fide resident of Diepkloof. She was entitled to the documents and was ordered to go to the "pass office," where she stood in queues for close to a week, missing school day after day. She was then issued with a piece of paper that directed her to go to another office, where her application was to be made and where she was to be photographed.

One whole year went by with the child waiting for her book. She would go to the "offices" on the appointed day and would always be told to come back the next. Then one day Nozipho was informed that all her journeys had been in vain, because she was an "unknown person" in the Pretoria Births and Deaths Registration Office. This was because some fifteen years ago some careless official had given her a birth certificate with the wrong number and that before her application could succeed she had to go to the "Bantu Affairs Commissioner's" office in Johannesburg, and have the number on her birth certificate corrected.

And so began another pilgrimage of misery for my child. When the number was finally corrected, weeks later, the girl found that she had to reapply for her reference book and once more go backwards and forwards from office to office to office . . .

8

Youth in Crisis

Like the older black generation the present day black youth is in a state of shock; a severe identity crisis. It is confused and direction-less and in search of something — anything whatsoever onto which to cling in order to gain spiritual equilibrium. The savage, reckless aggression displayed by black children all over South Africa is but a manifestation of this great spiritual turmoil.

Our children cannot help feeling bitter and confused, caught as they are between a dying black culture on the one hand and a ravenning and blindly destructive white culture on the other. Our children cannot help being enraged because again and again in South African history books, they read things that ridicule, belittle and humiliate the black race.

In the privacy of their homes they are told to honour the memory of their ancestors, and they see their parents making sacrifices to the ancestral spirits. They also participate in these ceremonies and rituals and then at school they are taught that those ancestors were nothing but Godless savages and bloodthirsty tyrants who some merciful white God handed over to the white man to be shown the way. Our children are taught outright lies like the one to the effect that when Jan Van Riebeeck[103] came to the Cape to build a provi-sion station for ships bound for India, the interior of the Cape Province was bare of black people and that the only people who lived there were Bushmen and Hottentots.[104] The children are told this, in spite of overwhelming archeological proof to the contrary, and this in spite of recorded history such as the Portuguese sailors who, in the 15th century, reported having found Nguni speaking black people near the mouth of the Fish River, who sold them food known to be a traditional Zulu bread made from fresh maize ground and then boiled in water. This incident with the Portuguese occurred almost two hundred years before Van Riebeeck landed at the Cape.

Today the white education officials repeatedly urge black parents to exercise more authority over their children, despite that over the last thirty years or more the governments of South Africa have been laying down law after law, rule after rule, and regulation after regulation, whose cumulative effect has been the obliteration of not only what little authority the black parents had over their children, but also the tearing apart and destruction of the very woof, weft and fibre of black family life itself.

To understand why, let us dig deeper into the traditions and culture of Africa's black people. Anyone who has ever studied African family life closely and intimately will tell you that the traditional black family is an extremely complex structure consisting, of relatives, and relatives of relatives, each one of whom plays an extremely important part in ensuring stability of the basic family unit — which consists of the husband, wife (or wives) and children.

According to western culture it is the sole duty of the husband and his wife to bring up their children properly, and either succeed or fail in this most important duty; but this is not the case with a black African family where you find various relatives playing a permanent, daily and intimate role in assisting the husband and his wife or wives in the task of bringing up their children. In western culture, an erring child knows it only has two parents to face. While in Africa wayward children find themselves confronted by four to six relatives in addition to their parents, and each one of those relatives, the children know, has the same authority over them their natural parents have.

Among blacks you can see that bringing up a child is a communal effort shared by many relatives on both the mother's side and on the father's side, and this has made bringing up of children an easy duty for the parents and gives the child support on all sides.

One unusual thing about the African family is that an African child has only one set of uncles, those on his or her mother's side, who are known in Zulu as the *omalume*, a term which literally means "teachers" or "instructors."

The brothers of the child's father are not called *malume* but rather *baba-omncane;* that is "lesser father." The child's lesser father has the same powers over the child that its real *baba* or father has.

Our people believe in a Godhead that consists of three or four people, namely God the Father, God the Mother, God the Son — who was also the Sun-God — and God the Tree of Life. The Tree of Life is known to the Zulus as the *Simikade* tree, which is said to hold up the sky and to have its roots deep in the nether regions. In Zulu, God the Father is known as *Nkulunkulu,* a name that ignorant anthropologists always confuse with that of our first ancestor *Khulukhulwana.*

God the Mother is known as *Nomkhumbulwana* or *Nomcubulwana* the Earth Mother, and God the Son is known as *Mvelinqangi,* a name that means THE FIRST BORN OF THE ONE WHO APPEARED FIRST. Unlike western people who pray directly to the Almighty, black people in Africa choose rather to pray to God through the spirits of their forefathers — the so-called ancestral spirits — whose duty it is to act as a link between humanity on earth and God in Heaven.

Our people make monthly, and sometimes even weekly, sacrifices of goats, chickens and cattle to the ancestral spirits throughout southern and central Africa; but they never dare sacrifice anything to God because that would, in their view, be the height of blasphemy and insolence. God owns every animate and inanimate thing that there is on earth, and you would not dare take God's property and later offer it to God as a gift.

We consider the ancestral spirits not to be all powerful beings but rather to be human beings like ourselves who have been removed by death from this earthly plane of ours, but who, nevertheless, are still subject to the needs, moods and appetites to which we earthlings are subjected. This is why we make offerings of food and drink to them, to keep them well fed and content and ever prepared to deliver our prayers to the All-Highest in Heaven. We praise our ancestral spirits when things go right and curse them bitterly when things go wrong and thus they serve both as messengers and as scapegoats, because none of us is allowed to blame God for not having heard our prayers when we fail to receive what we prayed for. We rather blame the ancestors for having either refused to relay our prayers for some reason or for having not heard

49

us properly.

We believe the ancestral spirits, although now one with the immortals in the land of the gods, love this world of ours because it is the only world with food and drink and because the gods in their land as well as other immortals know neither hunger nor thirst, love nor hate. So the ancestral spirits love to continue living in this world of ours, usually living through us as parasites just as the isona weed lives through the maize-plant whose life-juices it sucks.

According to the mythology of all our people it was God the Son and God the Mother who created the earth and all we see upon it, and it is because of this that our people regard the woman and all female creatures as being sacred and greater spiritually than the man and all male creatures. It is also because of this that our people regard the child as a sacred creature, a creature beyond all tribal, racial and religious barriers, a creature to be loved, protected, guided and cherished by anybody anywhere.

It may surprise you to learn that Zulus refer to a child by a name which also means a *chief,* a *prince* or a *sovereign* — *umntwana.* In Zulu a male child is known as *umntwana wo mfana* or simply *umfana,* while a girl is known as *umntwana we ntombazane* or simply *Ntombazane.*

The black people of southern and central Africa as well as parts of eastern Africa refer to a woman by a remarkable name whose meaning is the same regardless of which language the speaker uses. The name means *the sprinkler of the seed* or *the broadcaster of the seed.* In Zulu the word for an adult, married woman is *umfazi* a word that is born of the verb *faza,* which means *to sow, broadcast* or *to sprinkle.* In Sotho and in Tswana, the name for a woman, a mature woman, is *mosadi,* which means *seed person.*

In Tswana and in Sotho, a man is known as *monna,* a name whose meaning is *the one sitting down* or *the static one.* A man in Zulu is called *indoda,* a word that merely means *a penis.* Thus, if you ask a Zulu woman rudely where her husband is you say: *indoda yakho iphi?* This literally means *the penis of yours it is where?* You will notice that here the man is not referred to as *him* but rather as an *it.*

All these and many other revelations prove that women and children hold a very high position in African society. The man is held to be woman's spiritual inferior, being merely the protector and guardian of both the woman and the child. The man was seen as the expendable protector of the woman and her children, who often lost his life in the carrying out of his duties, thus leaving the woman to continue with the task of preserving the family, the tribe and the race. While the man was still alive however he was honoured with titles and with power that were actually more symbolic than real, but beyond all that he was simply a protector, a provider and nothing else.

According to the culture of all tribes in southern Africa a conqueror who has attacked a tribe and crushed it in battle was not allowed to inflict the same sort of humiliation upon the defeated tribe's womenfolk that he was inflicting upon the surviving menfolk. He was expected by the ancient laws to spare the defeated tribe's women and children and to treat them decently regardless of what he chose to do with the menfolk. It was because of this ancient rule that black people saw the white authorities' intentions of extending the pass laws to black women in the late 1950s and early 1960s as a sacrilege that had to be resisted. It is this belief that lay behind the great protest marches by black women in 1918 and which also lay behind the Sharpeville tragedy of 1960.

Coming back to the children: as I have said before, in our people's eyes a child has always been viewed as a sacred person. It is everybody's duty to guide, cherish and protect a child, because a child, is seen as a neutral person who, like a woman and like a witchdoctor or sangoma, is above tribal barriers.

Some warlike tribes in Africa, the Zulus included, had a custom of capturing as many enemy children as possible during forays into the territory of other tribes, to bring them back with captured enemy cattle and rear them as members of the tribe. Sometimes a warrior tribe, which found continuous warfare had thinned its numbers, would launch special raids into the lands of enemy tribes to capture women and children.

Any adult who saw children doing something wrong such as fighting among themselves, torturing a bird or an animal, or carelessly allowing goats or cattle to invade a maize field and destroy the crop was compelled by law to stop and punish those children. That person was either severely reprimanded or fined heavily by the local chief if he or she failed to do so.

I vividly recall two incidences that happened to me as a child. The first of them was when, during one one hot day in late Spring, I treated myself to a rather heavy dinner of roasted chicken and boiled fresh maize while out in the veld herding goats. I then rested in the cool shade of a thorn tree and was soon fast asleep. The goats, probably seeing me asleep, must have conspired together to raid a nearby maize field and were soon feasting right and royally on the young green maize.

I was rudely awakened by a total stranger who first asked me whether I was alive or dead and on receiving my trembling answer that I was alive, he took off his belt and gave me the biggest hiding of my eight-year-old life, and after he had completed his tribal duty, he helped me to drive the goats out of the maize, got on his donkey and went on his way.

It was my duty as a herdboy to go and report my carelessness to the owner of the maizefield, Mfeka, and my uncle, who decided that as the stranger had already punished me, my hide needed no further tanning. My uncle paid Mfeka the amount of ten shillings and sixpence for damages to his crops, and that was the end of the matter.

On the second occasion I was alone on top of a koppie[105] among the rocks making clay oxen, when I hit upon an idea that was to get me yet another thrashing. Ruling our district at this time was a very colourful chief, Manzolwandle, the son of Cetshwayo, who was famous for his tremendous appetite and girth; and I decided to make a clay portrait of this great chief. I immediately got to work, modelling a small image of the chief sitting upon his royal stool and smiling. When the statuette was completed, I decided to add four more people sitting in a semi-circle at the feet of the clay image of the chief, and once more I decided to portray living people . . . some of the people who lived in the chief's great kraal.[106]

It was not long before my work attracted the attention of some of the locals who climbed the koppie to admire the work. The crowd attracted two elders, who obviously had no appreciation of art whatsoever and who proceeded to warm me up nice and proper, accusing me of practising witchcraft. They said no one on earth, short of using witchcraft, could have so accurately portrayed not only the chief but also his servants in clay. After the beating, I was hauled off to the chief's village after being told that my offence was very grave indeed and that I might be lucky to get away with my life once I was brought to Manzolwandle.

When I was brought before the mighty chief I was almost dead with terror and pain and I saw, through a mist of unbelievable anguish, the damning evidence in the form of the clay statuettes being placed before the chief by the two elders. Time seemed to stand still while the huge chief examined my handiwork, and then I wet my khaki shorts as Manzolwandle rose to his feet and walked slowly towards me. Reaching down with a huge hand he hauled me to my feet, took one look at the front of my shorts and roared with laughter.

"Hawu ! UCetshwayo yini? Uyazichamela, mfana ?" roared the chief, his smile as broad as a spring sunrise — "And who told you, boy, that I, Manzolwandle was a beast to be feared?"

The chief turned upon the men who had brought me before him and rebuked them for having thrashed me. No child should ever be thrashed for doing things of beauty, he said. Then he turned to my aunt's husband and commanded him to see to it that I got a good education at the local mission school. He added that the work I had done in clay would one day make me a great man if I continued with it. He told the elders that he had seen white people buy clay and wooden images from black people in the streets of Eshowe and Durban and that they must not act like fools in future.

He then ordered that I be given a cock and a hen from his huge flock of chickens as a gift and ordered me to go home and rest for the day.

When the time comes for a child to learn about the facts of life, such as sex, it becomes the duty of the child's malume to either teach the child about sex, or to send him or her to an initiation school for lessons. African people see it as wrong and dangerous for parents to teach their children about sexual matters; they feel that it could have the effect of losing the parents' credibility in the eyes of the children — because if you, as a parent, have spent years telling your children they were brought into this world by a great white bird or by a little old woman with one leg bigger than the other, the children will lose respect for you if you suddenly turn around and tell them the truth. Thus, it is the duty of either the malume or the grandmother or grandfather to teach the children.

When a Zulu girl is about to get married she always pays a ritual visit to her uncle's home, about a fortnight before her wedding day, where she receives ritual gifts of various kinds — these she receives with her eyes shut. This ceremony is called the "cimeza," which means the "eyes closed" ceremony. After the ceremony, the uncle and his wife or wives give the girl important tips about lovemaking, baby-care, looking after children and looking after a husband.

Under African traditional law there is no "coming of age" for a child, as is known in western tradition, when a child reaches its twenty-first birthday and is to be hence-forth regarded as an adult with full control over his or her life. Under African tradition you remain a child under the full control of your parents for as long as they are alive.

Now, with the coming of great township complexes such as Soweto, with their draconian and brutally enforced influx-control laws and permit regulations, it becomes impossible for black residents in these townships to live with their relatives who traditionally assisted them in bringing up their children. Thus the extended family, already in its death throes, was dealt one final mortal blow. To our people, being members of one family means either living together under the same roof or in dwellings adjacent to each other.

In the old townships such as Alexandra and Pimville, the members of the family are nearly always found living together in a number of adjacent shacks . . . sharing food, drink and sometimes even clothing and money; and generally making life easier for each other in many other ways. This is one of the most important reasons why black people refuse to move out of squatter-camps, such as Crossroads in the Cape, to townships such as Khayelitsha.

In the squatter camps people live in extremely unhygienic conditions indeed, *but they are free.* Free of the brutal township bureaucracy, free of the unnatural regimentation and free to live with the members of their families they choose, without having to apply to some office for a "permit." It is only in places like Crossroads that blacks find the opportunity to practice free-enterprise, because in such places, one can start a small business selling fruit or vegetables at a bus-stop and rapidly graduate to a small corrugated iron stall next to one's home-shack, without once having to go through South Africa's soul-strangling red-tape.

Some of the wealthiest men in Soweto began as businessmen in the squatter camps and shanty-towns of the fifties, selling offal, potatoes and even cheap cosmetics at bus stops or from house to house. In a squatter camp the black man finds it — ironically — easier to live the life he wants, a life that is denied him in the townships. He can live with whom ever he chooses, he can have two or three wives, and he can start a thriving backyard business, which he is discouraged from doing in the townships. In townships, blacks find they are not allowed to keep livestock, such as goats, cattle and pigs, but in a squatter camp they can do it without anyone saying nay to them.

In the 1950s, 1960s and 1970s, laws were passed and enforced by township authorities, in townships such as Soweto, which plunged to the depths of shortsightedness and stupidity. One of these laws was that children over sixteen years of age were no longer allowed to live in the same house as their parents, but had to go out and find their own accommodation elsewhere. This was crazy because no single people were allowed to have houses in the township, and in order to have a house of his own the "over-age" child had to find a wife and get married.

Thus thousands of young blacks were forced by township regulations into marriages for which they were not prepared, marriages that soon ended in desertion or in divorce and after one, two or even three children had been born.

This law, rule or regulation, or whatever you choose to call it, is directly behind the burgeoning population of the townships. It has been one of the causes of deep misery to a countless numbers.

There is another rule that I revealed before the *Cillie Commission of Inquiry*[107] into the 1976 Soweto riots. This rule was enforced by the West Rand Administration Board in townships such as Diepkloof and Meadowlands. All children over sixteen years of age had to have separate resident's permits known as "lodgers permits," and had to pay rent to the local superintendent's office for "living in their father's house."

This rule was, and still is, the cause of severe friction between children and parents in the townships. Black children see themselves as independent adults, free of all parental restraint. That they were paying rent in their parents' house, and emboldened by this law, some sons and daughters actually assaulted their aged parents and drove them out of their homes. *Sic Transit Gloria Africae . . . .*

If the South African Government is sincere in its reform programme it must immediately restore to black parents the authority it took away. Without parents having a firm control over their children, the Government will lose these South African children to the communist force of revolution and anarchy much sooner that it expects.

Make no mistake, of all the white governments, it was the present

Government that held sway over this country, and did the most damage to our family life. Thus, it is duty-bound to put that damage right and quickly.

9

Education in Crisis

Originally, the school was intended to be an extension of a child's home, and teachers and parents were supposed to work together hand in hand at the holy task of moulding today's children into tomorrow's upright citizens. Instead, over the years, in many instances and in many ways, parents and school authorities have drifted slowly apart. Instead of working together they often work against each other to the detriment of the child's education and development as a thinking human being.

The schools have ceased to be places of education, they have ceased to be places with a human face and soul and instead they have become rather like factories in some distant nightmare, turning out long rows of identical pre-programmed robots to serve a human race that has long vanished from the face of the globe. God and religion have been expelled from schools and other places of education, yet for thousands of years, religion and instruction have gone hand in hand.

The greatest mistake the South African Government ever made, where black education is concerned, was putting an end to mission schools. Believe you me, these schools would have acted as a strong buffer against the violence that has torn apart thousands of black schools in many parts of South Africa.

One very important and little know fact is that in the black township Catholic schools, and other schools belonging to certain churches, were free of unrest for many years. The children in these schools risked life and limb again and again to attend school faithfully each day, even at the height of the rioting, and it took savage acts of intimidation by militant student organizations to finally break their resistance.

In the Diepkloof suburb of Soweto, there are two schools standing next to each other separated only by a concrete wall. One of these schools is a state school, known as "Junior Secondary." It is a school that has been closed down many times because it is a hotbed of militant activity. The second school, on the contrary, is a vast, beautifully built, and well cared for school called "Holy Cross," which is a school run by the Catholic Church with a number of white nuns and black nuns.

Throughout the bloody 1976 riots and even the bloodier 1984 riots the "Holy Cross" school remained an island of calm in the midst of a hideous storm of petrol bombs, stones, tyres, tear-gas and bullets. It remained so until late in 1985 when a horde of activists launched a direct assault upon it, badly injuring a child with a cane knife and forcibly dispersing the Catholic scholars.

The activists threatened to burn down the school and all the souls within it, unless the "Holy Cross" children toed the militant line. Two of my children were scholars in the school at the time of the incident, and one of them, Theresa, was hit by a brick, thrown by an activist. To this day my child still has trouble moving her right arm.

The main reason why the children studying at the "Holy Cross" school risked all to attend classes, even during days of worse violence, was because of their respect for the nuns in the school and their faith in Jesus Christ. Again and again when I asked children studying at "Holy Cross," why they insisted on going to school even on days of extreme danger, I always received one answer, from not only my two little daughters, but their school friends as well, that *"I Jesu uzosivikela, Baba — Jesus will protect us, father."*

Today children have lost all respect for their teachers and have lost the will to go to school. Many unpleasant things done by school authorities to children lie directly behind the present violence and the boycotts and stayaways. One of these is the habit of sending children home if they do not have certain kinds of books or do not have certain items of uniform. The child is usually sent from school with orders not to return until his or her parents have provided the items required. This sort of treatment crushes the child's spirit and is a thousand times more painful than a caning. This causes the child to miss days, even weeks, of school lessons, and it creates an impression in the child's mind that it is being used as a pawn in a feud between the school authorities and the parents.

This ugly, medieval practice is found in schools all over South Africa and the national states, and could only have been invented by a follower of Marquis de Sade.[108] In the early days, mission school authorities were dead set against all forms of wastefulness; economy was the watchword in all things, and in those days, if a child had bought an exercise book the teacher would see that the book was kept clean and that he or she used every line. No space or page would be left wastefully unwritten upon. The children carried only a few exercise books to school; all of them tidily and thriftily used. Nowadays hundreds of black children are burdened by an incredible forty or more exercise books and notebooks in addition to the mathematics books and other textbooks required. Some of these exercise books only get used once, and once only for the whole year the child is in school.

There was also another practice, now thankfully controlled in many schools in our townships, a practice which greatly destroyed the dignity of the teachers in the eyes of the school children. Teachers became freelance salespeople who received large commissions by compelling their pupils to buy school uniforms from certain shops only.

The teacher would write a note to the parent saying that the child required new socks or a jersey, and that the item was obtainable at such-and-such a shop. The idea was that the parent should take this note to the shop indicated and present it to the shop assistant when making the purchase, so that the manager of the shop would know which teacher sent the customer and thereby pass on the commission.

I hope and trust that as South Africa's reform speeds up all these and other ugly things will become things of a best forgotten past, and that education will once more assume the importance and dignity it once had so many grey years ago. I pray to God beyond the stars that I may live just long enough to see the teaching profession restored to the dignity and the respect it once enjoyed.

There was once a time, when I was about twenty summers old when teachers were deeply respected by everyone, because teachers were more than mere teachers in those days. A teacher was a symbol of wisdom, a symbol of strength, and a symbol of the nation's hope; but not anymore.

I wish that all that beauty could be restored to this ancient profession. No matter how much man advances along the highway of knowledge, no matter how many staggering and breathtaking advances man may make he will require teachers, even if they one day will be robots made of stainless steel.

10

The Soweto Riots

Let me now speak about something that happened in Soweto in 1976 — namely the Soweto Riots. When these riots broke out on that bright Wednesday — a beautiful day on which there was not a single cloud to be seen in the winter skies — the media told the world the cause of the riots was that the South African Government had forced black children to take certain lessons in the Afrikaans language.

This was a very simplistic explanation for a highly complex problem. The people in the townships, notably our youth, speak more Afrikaans each day than English and use a language that our people call "Tsotsi-taal." This language is the lingua-franca of the townships, it is the means of communication between young people of different tribes, and even different races, and it consists of about seventy percent Afrikaans and Afrikaans slang and about thirty percent Bantu and Bantu slang.

A Soweto boy using this language can communicate not only with a boy from another tribe but also with a coloured boy from the Cape where a high percentage of Afrikaans is spoken. If a young Zulu man calls his girl friend he'll say "ntombi, woza-la," which means "maiden, come here." But if he uses Tsotsi-taal he will say "zwakala-hier cherie." The words "hier" and "cherie" are Afrikaans; "hier" being pure Afrikaans for "here" and "cherie" being Afrikaans slang for a young girl. The word zwakala is Bantu slang for "be heard" or "reveal yourself."

So what then was the cause for the 1976 tragedy if black people in the townships speak Afrikaans nearly every day of their lives, albeit in this horribly outlandish mixture known as "tsotsi-taal." The cause of the 1976 riots is to be found at the roots of the African traditions. According to the culture of the tribes, a nation's language is a living entity, and if a person wants to learn the language of a people, he or she must not be compelled by anyone to do so, but rather they must do it out of free choice as part of their attempts to understand these people whose language they are learning — and thus to be able to communicate fully with them.

The moment you start to force a person in Africa to speak your language you are degrading that person in the most terrible way, because only slaves were ever compelled to speak the language of their captors and their masters.

When in older times an African king discovered a deposit of, say, copper ore in the territory of his tribe, and he wanted manpower to exploit this deposit, he would raid the land of another tribe and capture all its powerfully built men. These slaves would do the dangerous mining of the ore, but before being put to work, they had to first learn the language of their captors . . . in order that the captors could issue commands to them freely.

The slaves were beaten and sometimes tortured to force them to learn the words of their captors, and sometimes the king would go to the extent of gripping each captured slave by the nose, and pinching the nostrils together — forcing the mouth open — the king would spit into the slave's mouth. The idea behind this bizarre act was to put some of the saliva from the captors into the mouths of the slaves in the hope that he would be quick in learning the language.

So when the Government decided to make Afrikaans compulsory in black schools, it was offensive to African traditions. No person should ever be forced to learn another person's language.

This is all it was and well over six hundred people died needlessly in the riots. One can only hope and pray before God that a tragedy of this type is never again repeated in South Africa. We have never tried to understand or study each other to any depth, and thus I am afraid that unless this is done, such tragedies will happen again and yet again.

11

The House That Never Was

What little change the Government tried to initiate after the 1976 riots was piecemeal, haphazard, and time-consumingly slow and was initiated through the same discredited and thoroughly detested organizations that brought about the riots in the first place, namely the Department of Bantu Education,[109] the Bantu Administration Boards[110] and the Urban Bantu Councils.[111]

It was known to all who lived in the townships that the Bantu Administration Boards and the Urban Bantu Councils were riddled with corruption. The administration boards, especially, were nests of old, rigid-minded and aggressive white officials of both the conservative and ultra-conservative stripe; men whose attitude towards blacks had not changed since the Second World War and who had seen service under men like Malan, Strijdom and Verwoerd.

These elderly white officials saw no reason why they should change their "time-tried" ways of dealing with blacks and many of them pooh-poohed any new improvement in the status quo that the Government tried to make, saying the Government was "going soft" on blacks and doing "too much" for them. These men went out of their way to do everything to frustrate the Government's aims.

Even at the height of the unrest in 1976 there were Administration Board and Urban Council officials dabbling in petty corruption, and who were making nonsense of Mr Piet Koornhof's efforts to bring about home-ownership for blacks under the thirty-year[112] and ninety-nine year leasehold schemes.[113]

While my family and I were living on a farm in Natal, after the destruction of our previous home in Soweto by radicals in 1976, I was told a law had been passed that would enable black people in Soweto and other townships to own their houses under the thirty-year leasehold scheme. I decided to buy my house, which had since been repaired, in Diepkloof Township. I bought it for cash hoping to save money and improve it; thus creating a secure future for our children.

When I returned with my family to Diepkloof to the house I now assumed was mine, we were constantly being subjected to almost nightly terrorization by people who would fire a number of shots from a small-calibre firearm through our kitchen window. One night my wife and I decided it was not safe to live there and we moved our children to another place. It was then that our troubles started. People arrived and said they wanted to buy my house; that they had been told by someone in the township manager's office my house was up for sale. Again and again I told these people to leave and that my house was not for sale to them or anyone else.

Some weeks after this I received a notice from the township manager's office that I owed some forty-two rand in unspecified "arrears," and that I had to pay this amount within a stated period or face eviction. I then began to notice something very odd and sinister about this notice. I could not have been in arrears because I had bought my house for cash; in fact I had accidentally over-paid by about eighty rand and this extra money was yet to be refunded.

I knew from bitter experience that black township residents stood no chance against officials in the township manager's office, and that if they accuse you of owing it is always better to pay.

The delivery of the threatening document had been deliberately delayed until the last possible moment, so as to make it impossible for me to pay the amount demanded. And because of this I appealed to the Director of the Soweto Parks and Recreation Department, the department that controlled our traditional museum village[114] in the centre of Soweto. The Director telephoned the township manager to lodge a vigorous protest about the treatment I was receiving, and the upshot of this was that the township manager gave me a day's grace in which to pay. When I arrived to pay the township manager advised me to sell my house — to "flog your house" as he put it.

Some days later after this ugly episode, I read a newspaper report that the thirty-year leasehold scheme was nothing but a dirty racket. The newspaper revealed that any person who bought a house under this scheme could be deprived of the house by the local township manager if he, among other things, "owed money." So that was it! These officials had been trying to "frame" me into a position where they could legally seize my house so they could sell it to some black man, one of them had "known for years"!

I was to learn much later that there were people in various townships who had lost houses they had bought under this scheme and under circumstances almost identical to those under which I came close to losing my children's home. This story did not have a happy ending. There was much, much more misery I had to endure in an attempt to provide for my children's future.

Exactly what was the meaning of the Byzantine rigmarole? Can you first sell a man a second-hand car and then turn around and tell him he only owns the body and the engine and not the wheels and petrol-tank; and that he must pay you yet more money before he can drive away and call that car his own?

A foul stench of dishonesty still hangs over the entire black home-ownership business and the whole thing has the appearance of a gigantic Machiavellian hoax, intended to deceive the outside world and to bleed black home-buyers in the townships of as much money as possible. The various schemes were created in order to give black people something to be proud of and something they would defend with their lives against rampaging radical arsonists and vandals — homes they could call their very own. But somewhere along the line the whole thing has become defiled and distorted by scheming white officials and thieving black councillors.

And now, instead of creating a content, home-owning black middle-class, the scheme has embittered and shocked many who trusted the Government's word and desperately wanted to possess something we could improve and of which we could be proud. Black people who buy homes and establish businesses in South Africa are literally risking death at the hands of so-called ANC activists by doing so because they are seen by these murderers as "sell-outs" who are "collaborating with the system" and who are therefore prime candidates for the car-tyre "necklace" treatment.

I do not know whether the South African Government realizes that although we black people have no meaningful vote in this country, some of us choose to vote with creative hands for a better future; and that we choose to show our confidence in a shining future by the homes we buy and the businesses we establish.

By not preventing all this bitterness the Government is actually cutting its own throat and endangering the country the white voters have entrusted it with, more surely than either the ANC or any other organization can endanger it.

South Africa's greatest and deadliest enemy is HERSELF and not some raging terrorist bands skulking in the bush beyond her borders. It is my wish that one day this country tear out its heart by the roots, chop it to pieces and examine it under a microscope . . . it would be shaken by the evil it shall see crawling there.

12

Images of Capitalism . . .

Despite all the talk of reform, black people in South Africa still experience cruelty and degradation in many places. They experience it in government offices, in township manager's offices, in post offices, in banks, in police stations and — God be my witness — in clinics and in hospitals where they go in search of help in times of illness and injury.

I do not know just how many times in the past five years or so, I have written angry letters of protest to the public relations officers of some banks and building societies in Johannesburg . . . after I or a friend or relative had been subjected to unprovoked and insulting behaviour by a teller. Such has been my personal experience of this that I want the whole world to know that in certain branches of the well-known banks, with international parents, are to be found some of the most racist and rudest tellers, both black and white alike. And it is so obvious that in some parts of Johannesburg blacks avoid certain "racist banks" where staff refuse to serve them or they feed them all kinds of confusing nonsense.

It is common practice in South Africa for employers of black labour, such as various city and town councils, the railways and other large concerns, to compel their employees to take out bank or building society savings books and be paid through them. I do not know exactly what the reason behind this is, but I do know that it exposed poorly educated and even illiterate black people to all manner of ill-treatment and hardship.

Three years ago one of the major building societies in Johannesburg decided to cancel the savings accounts of thousands of railway and Soweto Council employees. This caused heartrending pain to thousands of black people, who had saved a little money in special savings accounts, and caused them to lose their meager savings. These people simply threw away their savings books in anger and disgust, not knowing exactly what was taking place. I will not defile this book by naming the building society; but let me say this: It is high time all the financial institutions in South Africa wake up to their responsibilities towards the people of this land — especially blacks.

Banks and building societies are prime targets for communist propaganda — anti-capitalism — in South Africa and if they care to blunt this propaganda they must start treating *all* people equally. They too have a part to play in the new reform process in this country and they must start to play their part properly or face the contempt and censure of all thinking people. Some of these financial institutions are supported by parent institutions in Europe and the USA, and they must be made aware of the fullest implications of this fact. They must refrain from doing anything that might contribute towards the West disinvesting completely from South Africa.

13

Images of the Medical Institutions

Every person who reads a newspaper knows the incident of tuberculosis (TB) is on the upswing in the townships as well as in the rural areas in South Africa. Although some "experts" have blamed everything from "black ignorance" to the present "economic climate," the basic cause of this upswing is first and foremost the lack of proper communication between the medical authorities and victims of this disease — not to mention the shabby and often shameful way in which these same medical personnel treat the unfortunates who have contracted this foul scourge.

Black people regard TB in the same light that ancient Hebrews regarded leprosy. A horrible disease visited upon the sufferer by some angry god as a result of immoral behaviour committed by the sufferer. They believe for instance, especially in Natal, that men who contract TB broke the great taboo that forbids men from making love to women still in mourning. And that women who contract this disease are those who have either been poisoned by jealous rivals, who have been made love to by a *tokoloshe* — an evil spirit. All black sufferers from TB become guilt-ridden and filled with deep embarrassment and self-pity.

Some try to hide all this under a thin blanket of fatalism and almost annoying cheerfulness. Such people require to be handled with the deepest sensitivity and care by people who know all the finer nuances of traditional African culture and religion, by people who are shamefully absent in the ranks of white or black medical personnel qualified to deal with such "cases."

One thing that turns sufferers away from the TB clinics and hospitals, is the weird symbol used by the South African National Tuberculosis Association (SANTA). This symbol closely resembles the traditional African symbol for death, a symbol that is feared by thousands of rural blacks as the sign of the deepest misfortune.

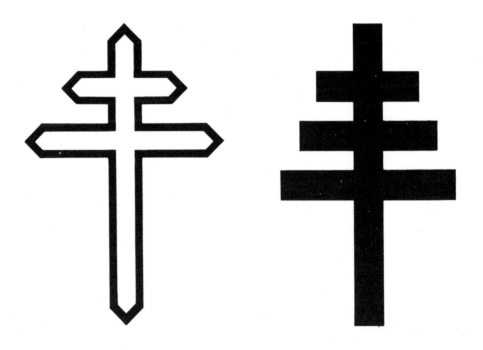

The Cross of Lorraine (left) — the symbol used world-wide by anti-tuberculosis organizations and by the South African National Tuberculosis Association (SANTA); and (right) the traditional symbol of death, which is painted outside kraals as a warning.

Ignorant medical people go out of their way to ridicule black traditional beliefs and fears expressed by TB sufferers. They will take a pair of scissors and cut off any charms the sufferer may be wearing, in the form of consecrated strings around the wrists or the necks of victims of any serious disease. What these doctors do not know, and rarely care to know, is that it is a deadly mistake — deadly for the black patient that is — to destroy any charms the patient may be wearing, and to ridicule the patient's beliefs and fears. Rather one should see these charms, beliefs and fears as a God-sent lever, which could be used by any person who knows African tradition and religion to gain the patient's co-operation and rapid recovery.

Ignorance and cruel treatment of patients in hospitals must be stopped as part of the process of building a new South Africa. People must not dare pretend this ignorance and cruelty does not exist and is a figment of my corpulent imagination. I could write a whole book on this sort of thing; but I shall endeavour to let these examples suffice.

There are white doctors in South Africa who treat many black patients as dirt and not actually as a sick person in need of urgent help. I have often come into the hands of such monsters in the course of my adult life, and many times I have been victim to extremely offensive personal remarks these so-called physicians would never dare use on a white person.

One doctor told a colleague in my hearing that I was as "fat as a shithouse"; and to this unprovoked insult I retorted by saying that being as fat as a pit-latrine has its uses, because when I die I shall fertilize the earth with my body while he would pollute it with his scrawny carcass. I for one am not at all surprised that Steve Biko[115] received such foul treatment at the hands of the two doctors who were tending to his injuries. He was a handsome, hefty young black man, a real African chief figure. This extremely obscene attitude towards blacks, especially fat ones, has become such a long-standing fact of South African life that it has now percolated into the dirty minds of some black doctors and nurses in private surgeries and hospitals; and they are now slavishly aping the behaviour of their white "masters" and mentors and carrying it to extremes.

Early in 1975, I was working with an adze in the yard of my Diepkloof home and carving an image in pine of the Zulu king Shaka as part of the decorations for the traditional village we were building at the foot of the Oppenheimer Tower in the centre of Soweto. While I was working the adze slipped and struck me just below the left knee, opening an ugly wound . . . an accident I had suffered once before in the course of my career as a sculptor. The wound began to bleed furiously in spite of all I could do to stem the blood-flow. Luckily there arrived two white officials of the West Rand Administration Board in a small truck who immediately took me to the main Diepkloof clinic. There the two white men explained to the senior sister that I had been injured and I required urgent treatment. The sister took one look at me and told the two officials how dare they bring such a filthy looking person to this clinic and that I "needed a haircut."

This woman persecuted me so savagely and in such a loud and shrill voice that many heads turned in my direction and a wave of laughter filled the reception area. When I tried to defend myself the woman told me she was not interested in my excuses and that I was a nauseating sight. I simply got up and walked out — my wound gaping and unattended.

I remained in my house for two days and on the third day the two officials came to see me again and found me quite sick. They took me back to the same clinic and there the wound was stitched. I swore never to return to that place again, and when the wound knitted I asked my wife and another female sangoma to cut the stitches with a dressmaker's pair of scissors and pull them out with a small pair of wire-pliers, using disinfectant as a guard against possible infection.

The following year, 1976, the clinic was razed to the ground by rioting mobs . . . .

14

The Humiliation of Tri-Cam

Finally, another cause of the surging violence — one of the major causes — is one of vote. But not so much as not having a vote, but of being bitterly humiliated by the present South African Government's Tri-Cameral Parliament.[116]

Black violence and rage grew much worse after they saw coloureds and Indians going into parliament while their race was excluded. Many black racists regard Indians as interlopers who robbed black people of large tracts of land, especially in Natal, without having defeated them in open battle; and they regard the "pure" black race as being higher than the mixed blood of the coloured people.

Thus the Tri-Cameral Parliament was really a monumental blunder doomed to an even more spectacular failure than separate development ever was. It was a blunder because it created an impression in the minds of thousands of apolitical and law-abiding blacks that the Indians, the coloureds and the whites were ganging up on them for some sinister reason. And now this feeling of rejection is flowing from the hearts of thousands of black people in South Africa . . . people who were once law abiding citizens.

15

The Rise of Terror in South Africa

Now do you know why the existing South African Government's reform initiatives have come too late for a shockingly large majority of young black people. Their rage is now such that nothing the present Government says or does makes any impression upon their minds, and even things such as the scrapping of the Influx Control Laws and the Pass Laws, dramatic as they are, leave hundreds of blacks utterly cold and unimpressed.

The present Government refused to heed the bloody lesson of the 1976 riots; it refused to see, as many of us at grassroots-level saw, that those riots were a warning — a curtain raiser of much worse to come. Even the ominous findings of the Cillie Commission of Inquiry in 1976 failed to galvanize the Government into doing the right thing at the proper time.

What the Government failed to realize was that the very laws they laid down to enforce peace and order in South Africa, were actually doing much to promote disturbance and disorder. That, for example, laws such as the Suppression of Communism Act[117] was, far from suppressing communism, actually helping *to spread* it among the black youth, especially by making all people who had been "named" or house-arrested as communists become objects of pity as well as objects of hero-worship in the eyes of thousands of hero-hungry youths.

Black people believe in a saying: "That which my enemy dislikes

I must love, and that which he finds evil must therefore be good for me"; and it was because of this belief that black people began regarding all those men and women, some white, some black and some coloured or Indian — who fell foul of the Suppression of Communism Act and other similar acts in South Africa — as good people whose example and whose philosophy had to be followed. This is why today you find at some township funerals where riot victims are being buried the communist flag is flown openly in cold defiance of the law and of the Government.

Another law that backfired badly was the famous Terrorism Act[118] with its ninety-day detention clause, a law that was used by scores of aspiring "heroes of the black struggle" to gain instant recognition as "genuine black leaders" worldwide. The Terrorism Act had been designed as the harshest law on the pages of the law books of this country, a law that was intended to make any would be terrorist think twice before trying to emulate Che Guevara in the South African bush. But what the creators of this law did not realize was that many black people look upon suffering or even death for a cause that one has reason to regard as just, as one of the noblest goals that any person in this world can aspire to, and it would not be long before some of these blacks saw in this law and others like it a godsent means of reaching this goal with ease. It therefore became quite common to find many brilliant and well educated young men and women in our townships who had not been able to make a success of their lives, going out of their way to engineer their own detention under the Terrorism Act.

These young people joined subversive organizations and small radical groups and started doing, saying and even writing things they knew very well would eventually bring down the full wrath of the state upon their heads. When you speak to some of these young people you will find out that they only possess the sketchiest ideas of what the real aim of the groups and organizations they had joined really are, and that, furthermore, they really did not care to know. They had joined these radical groups and organizations not out of any firm conviction but rather as part of their ravelling search for recognition as people of some worth — both by their friends in South Africa and by the world at large.

Even at this very moment for any young person in the townships to have been detained under the Terrorism Act is a sign of high status; one that is looked upon as one of the black elite, a "comrade" in the noble company of the Mandelas,[119] the Sisulus[120] and the Bikos and other "heroes" and "heroines" of the black struggle.

South Africa is one of the many countries in the world where you find tens of thousands of young people who have nothing to live for, but much to get angry about and even to die for, and one thing their leaders do is recruit thousands of these purposeless youths and offer them a purpose for the first time in their lives — even if that purpose eventually turns out to be a violent death and an early grave.

youths and offer them a purpose for the first time in their lives — even if that purpose eventually turns out to be a violent death and an early grave.

A law ceases to be a law once law breakers start using it as an instrument of achieving those aims they would never have achieved had that law not been there. Nowhere is this more true than with some of South Africa's security laws, which, far from ensuring the safety of the State rather strengthened the cause of insurrection and ensured the State's downfall.

In dealing with black people the pre-reform leaders committed the mistake of showing intransigence where they should have shown flexibility and imagination. They sometimes moved slothfully when they should have moved with speed and alacrity and they sometimes displayed cold and unreasoning cruelty when they should have shown mercy and understanding. Thus they again and again played right into the hands of black demagogues "on the make," as they say in the USA, and lost not only the fight for the hearts and the minds of the black population, but also the sympathy of many people in the outside world.

But, who has not made mistakes in South Africa? It is true that the white man has made many mistakes in this country, but then so too has the black man. If the white man has at last decided to put right many things he did wrong in the past then the black man too must reform and do his share, because REFORM IS NOT A ONE-WAY ALLEY — IT IS A DOUBLE-LANE HIGHWAY.

Much has been said and written about apartheid that exists in South Africa between white and black, but no one has ever had the truthfulness, honesty and courage to expose and write about the shameful apartheid that exists between black and black, and the apartheid that many black leaders in South Africa and other parts of the African continent try to ignore and treat as if it does not exist; despite that black on black apartheid has claimed millions of victims in intertribal wars all over Africa. And it is this black on black injustice that I will discuss in the following few chapters.

16

Black on Black Apartheid

White on black apartheid has resulted in a lot of suffering and a few thousand deaths in the last forty years; but black on black apartheid has claimed the lives of millions and has caused untold suffering.

If you refuse to believe this, then please ask yourself just how many people died in the terrible Baluba versus Luluwa[121] wars that followed the succession of the Katanga Province from the rest of the then Belgian Congo, which had just been granted independence by the Belgian monarch.

Also ask yourself just how many people died in the Biafran War[122] when Colonel Odumegwu Ojwuku[123] tried to excise his oil rich country from a corrupt and unstable Nigeria? How many unknown and uncounted thousands of Bahutus[124] and Wattutsi[125] perished in the terrible intertribal massacres in Ruwanda-Urundi?[126] And just how many rotting bodies are there buried in the shallow graves of Uganda that the entire western world continues to ignore?

And do you know that in South Africa in the last four years more black people have been killed in the little publicized intertribal wars and so called "faction-fights," than have been killed in the much more publicized township violence.

What the world does not know or fails to acknowledge is that South Africa is faced with two conflict situations. The first of which is the well known "township unrest" and the second is the little known intertribal and interfactional clashes always accompanied by heavy loss of life, and which occur sporadically nearly every year in various parts of Natal — the most spiritually corrupt of South Africa's four provinces. So serious have these bloody clashes become that in 1984 police began to suspect there must be a "godfather" master-minding these clashes. A report in the Star newspaper in Johannesburg on June 9, 1984 stated that the South African Police were seeking a suspected master-mind who was behind the faction fights. The newspaper further reported that some sixty tribesmen had been killed in a clash in the Umbumbulu district of Natal.

That was in 1984, and since then other bloody battles have taken place in this area and all claimed an average of thirty lives.

In this year, 1986, there have been three bloody battles in this region of Natal and two of these were between the very same factions that slaughtered each other in 1984. A third clash occurred shortly afterwards. A more recent bloody fight between members of the Zulu and Pondo tribes resulted in the deaths of over sixty people and the flight of hundreds of people to Durban.

These intertribal and factional killings even take place — almost every month — in cities and in the single men's hostels and the mine compounds. Firearms, many of them home-made, are the principal weapons of the feuding tribesmen.

What I find particularly strange is that these clashes and murders mostly involve different Zulu factions, and that Zululand under the control of Chief Mangosuthu Buthelezi's[127] powerful Inkatha movement, which is dedicated to peace and reconciliation among all people in South Africa, cannot for some reason succeed in ending this disgraceful blood-letting, this needless mass murder.

What I find distressing is the people involved in all this killing are not communist fanatics, but simple tribesfolk who are quite amenable to traditional methods of settling feuds and other forms of dispute. Contrary to what so-called experts on Zulu culture say, faction fighting is nothing new to the Zulu people or to any other African people. Man is a quarrelsome creature by nature and in this the black man is no exception.

There is strong historical evidence that clan, factional and even intertribal feuds occurred among the Zulus in Natal long before the white man came to South Africa. But there were traditional and effective methods of ending these conflicts and reconciling the two quarreling enemies.

I can only conclude that there is no one in either KwaZulu or the leadership of Inkatha who remembers these time tried methods of settling conflicts and reconciling the combatants. This is very odd considering that during the Rhodesian war, leaders of one of the guerrilla armies came together and went through one of the old peace ceremonies, known as the *Usiko Lo Dengezi;* that is, the custom of the dengezi clay bowl.

The men who went through this ritual were Joshua Nkomo's Matabeles, a tribe of warriors who came from Zululand in the last century, and whose culture is the same as that of the Zulus.

In the dengezi ritual a medicinal brew is prepared in a small clay pot and then each one of the participants is ordered to make a little cut on the back of his hand, usually the left. They then let a few drops of blood fall into the mixture, and while this is being done the sacred dengezi, which is a small saucerlike clay vessel, is heated in the ritual charcoal fire. The dengezi is brought out of the fire and the medicinal mixture poured into it. The participants must then dip their fingers into the medicine and lick them quickly — and they must do so twelve times.

People who have taken part in a dengezi peace ritual look upon each other no longer as either friends or as comrades, but rather as brothers — children of one man — for they have together licked a medicine containing traces of each other's blood.

This ritual is one of the simpler peace ceremonies, and I am positive it could be used in KwaZulu to put an end to faction-fighting. I would most seriously suggest to Chief Buthelezi that his Inkatha movement act with all urgency to put an end to faction-fighting in Natal.

I say this because warring factions are a serious threat to the stability of Natal and they could be exploited by outside forces to South Africa's undoing. Is it not possible that one day an interfering outside power such as Libya could try to destabilize South Africa by arming the various Zulu factions with modern weapons, setting them at each other's throats? Should that happen the results would be appalling.

17

The Burning of People

South Africans of all races should do well to pay heed to my words when I say it is within the realm of possibility that some outside power may manipulate and arm the warring factions to create havoc and instability in this country. At this very moment there is something extremely disturbing and utterly disgusting that is going on in South Africa, particularly in the Lebowa homeland in the Transvaal, and that needs to be shouted at, hissed at and condemned by all decent God-fearing human beings throughout the world.

For the last ten years or so, a rapidly increasing number of completely innocent people have been burnt alive in Lebowa on the pretext that they were "witches" who had caused the deaths of other folk by using magical power to call down lightning to strike them. Lightning deaths are quite common in Lebowa and have been for many generations.

Throughout southern Africa black people firmly believe that lightning does not strike and kill a human being unless some "wizard" or "witch" has caused it to do so. There is some basis for this strange belief, but it is too lengthy to go into it in this book.

When the witch-burnings of Lebowa started some ten years ago the "witches" were only burnt to death after having been "sniffed out" by some quack witchdoctor; but now the whole terrible thing has passed into the hands of "comrades," thugs and activists of the ANC and the UDF, who are using it as a tool of mass political intimidation of the tribal people for political ends.

The burnings in Lebowa began at almost the same time as the Soweto Riots in 1976, and they have continued ever since. A steady stream of victims of gruesome murders, who are either tied to wooden stakes or locked inside huts before being cremated alive, has continued unabated and which remains largely unpublicized. People are burnt alive on the backs of stationary trucks and others are hacked down with axes and pangas before being doused with petrol and burnt.

Originally there was only one or two victims at a time, but as the years went by even triple burnings became common. Now all of a sudden the whole thing has changed dramatically as young political thugs take over. It was reported in a Johannesburg Sunday newspaper recently that in a part of the Lebowa homeland known as Sekhukhuniland, a band of local youths inspired by the UDF forced the inhabitants of a small village to point out those among them whom they regarded as "witches."

When they had done this forty-three innocent men and women were herded like cattle and taken to a high mountain and burnt to death, one by one, in a hollow among rocks.

These youths — who called themselves "comrades" a term favoured by all ANC and UDF killer gangs in townships such as Soweto — had begun by threatening the local chief with death if he tried to intervene or telephone the police, and they also put the wind up the tribal headmen who were forced to stand by helplessly together with the rest of the surviving villagers, while the incredible orgy of "witch burning" went on.

The innocent victims were done to death in the dreaded "necklace" method — a trade-mark of the ANC and the UDF, which consists of tying the victim's wrists and ankles together, hanging a car tyre around the victim's neck and then filling the tyre with petrol and setting the tyre alight. The victim dies a horrible, screaming and choking death, and once you have seen such a sight you lose all belief in God and in the decency of man.

I not only have seen such a sight twice in Soweto but was nearly numbered among the victims in 1976, when my home was attacked and burnt. It is said that the Lebowa burnings went on for many hours while the silent, fear-paralyzed village watched in incredulous horror.

Then the "comrades" returned from the mist-shrouded mountain for more victims. They seized a woman and burned her alive in front of her terrified husband just outside the gate of her home, and then they forced the husband to bury her in their backyard. Then the "comrades" went to find an aggressive old man named Phadima Kupa, who had been denounced as a wizard by an intimidated neighbour. They found him and made known their intentions to him, but cantankerous old Phadima refused to go to the high mountain to die, demanding rather that he be burnt to death in his favourite maize field were the "comrades" had siezed him as he was busy harvesting his maize.

Old Phadima was not the only member of his family to die on that day, a niece of his, Miss Ramatsimela Teka, had been confronted by the young killers in her home and told that she had been denounced a witch and must be prepared to meet her fate. The woman calmly handed the grandchild she had been feeding maize porridge to, to a friend, got up, dusted her dress with her hands and followed the "comrades" after saying to the weeping friends "please look after the child for me . . . my day has come."

Unknown to these communist inspired murderers the old man Phadima and Miss Teka have friends and relatives in Soweto, and it was these friends and relatives who went to Lebowa to find out about the courageous way in which the two elderly people had gone to their awful deaths. Then the bereaved relatives came all the way to Mafikeng in Bophuthatswana to tell me because I had known both Phadima and his niece personally.

PHADIMA IS DEAD. He was a living history book from whose lips I learned much about the history of the Northern Sotho people. Phadima, with whom I once went on a journey to see the strangest tree in the whole world, the most sacred tree in Africa growing in incredible majesty in the Eastern Transvaal, the Shivhakava tree,[128] of which there is none like it in all Africa and which must only be visited by those who have reached the highest peak of sanusiship.

This is how the ANC proposes to liberate South Africa . . . by murdering women of wisdom and men of light. Phadima and his niece were not "sell-outs" but mere peasants, belonging to the class of people of which the ANC and its communist friends in the Soviet Union daily claim to liberate and protect.

There is a high law — held in firm belief by black people in Africa — that states that it is a foul sacrilege and an unforgivable sin against the majesty of the Earth Mother for any person to burn a living human being alive because by so doing one denies that human being's soul the God-given right of being reborn as a human being. In the olden times any ruler who made the mistake of burning a person alive even by accident was given the choice of suffering the same fate, at his own hands. He was surrounded by his own warriors and ordered to go into his hut and burn himself to death, but should he refuse to set the hut alight a terminally ill old man or woman was found to carry out the deed before being returned home to die.

Contrary to so-called experts who claim to know black tradition "witch burning" is not traditional to the Lebowan people, or to any tribe in southern Africa. Under North Sotho or Tswana law, witches whose crimes had been proven beyond all doubt were either beheaded or thrown to their deaths from clifftops. Only the witch's home was set alight to destroy any tokoloshes or other familiars she may have kept in her home.

Also, no person was condemned to death on the testimony of one witchdoctor alone, and tangible proof in the form of poisons, bewitching dolls and other paraphernalia used in the witch's or wizard's evil rituals had to be produced before the chief and the entire tribe.

But there is more: In the olden days it was much more common for the accused witch or wizard to be punished by being exiled from the tribe, and a first offender was very often punished with a severe public flogging in order to free him or her of the evil spirit.

Under the ancient laws a person accused of being a witch had the right to challenge his or her accusers to a high ordeal, which he or she was also prepared to undergo, and the ordeal usually took the form of placing one's hands upon a sacred clay pot, which had been heated to a red glow, for a few moments without flinching.

The accused first underwent the ordeal, suffering severe burns on the hands as a result, and then challenged the accusers to do the same if they dared. Under ancient Zulu law the high ordeal took the form of the accused being taken to the seaside and made to stand waist-deep in the water. Should the sea sweep the accused away, he or she was judged as having been guilty, but should the sea hurl him or her onto dry land it was regarded as a sign of innocence and acquittal.

I wish I could tell you more, but tears fill my eyes at all this desecration of my people's religion and culture by communistic groups and organizations that seek to plunge my country and its people into the flames of Armageddon. My God, what kind of people are these who, while claiming to be our liberators, are slaughtering us? Why is South Africa dying while the whole world watches? My God, what will it take to make people see reason, what will it take to make them see that there will be no winners in the sort of war they are starting in South Africa?

By burning people alive, the ANC and the other acitivists are doing what amounts to mass intimidation of the black people in South Africa. And I want to warn the ANC here and now that if it does not cease, and cease immediately, its habit of torturing and burning black people alive in South Africa, be they simple tribes-folk or township residents, it is going to find itself being viewed as a sworn enemy by millions of blacks.

There are millions who still follow the Great Religion and the traditions of their forbears, and if this desecration continues the ANC and its cadres will no longer find shelter in kraals and villages in frontline countries such as Botswana, Zimbabwe and Lesotho, and they will move through those countries on their way to and from South Africa only at their direct peril. Although there are many different tribes in southern Africa, they are all bound together by the same high religion whose laws are the same.

18

The Dreams

Just as individuals fall victim to illness both physical and mental, then so do whole nations and whole races, and it may come as a surprise to you to learn that in old Africa the duty of a sanusi was not only to look after the health of individuals but also that of the entire tribe.

It was — and still is — the duty of the sanusi to monitor dreams over a set period of time, dreams dreamt by men and women of certain age-groups in various parts of the tribeland, and should he notice something common and odd in say a hundred dreams brought to him over a two month period by tribespeople from various parts of the land, then the sanusi realized there was something wrong with the spiritual health of the tribe.

He would then call an urgent secret gathering of all lesser healers and diviners and urge them to investigate the problems in depth and over a much wider area and report to him within one month. After the completion of the investigation the sanusi would then seek audience with the tribal chief and his elders and give them a full report of what he and the other healers had found; and then the chief would take appropriate action.

Let us say the sanusi and his colleagues had found that more and more people in the tribe were dreaming of fire, or dreams involving fire, during a measured period of time, then the chief would know that most of the tribe was suffering from some kind of deep rooted tension. It then became his duty as a chief to identify and erase the tension before it tore the tribe apart.

In 1974, I noticed a strange thing happening in black communities such as Soweto. The people became unusually tense, suspicious and aggressive, and weird rumours began spreading through townships such as Diepkloof and Orlando East, rumours that gave birth to extremely violent behaviour towards white doctors as well as black medical personnel travelling through the townships in clinic vehicles. It was rumoured that there was a group of white doctors who were going through the townships catching black children and giving them fatal injections. So persistent and intense became this rumour that children started running and hiding when they saw a vehicle with red crosses on it approaching.

And then one afternoon a hospital vehicle going through Diepkloof Zone Two was attacked by a crowd consisting mainly of hysterically screaming women and youths, and savagely stoned, for the white coated people inside had been wrongly identified as the people who were giving children fatal injections.

The driver of the vehicle lost control under the thundering hail of missiles and the vehicle careered into the brick wall of the old Zone Two Superintendent's office. Only the timely arrival of the police saved the occupants of the vehicle from a terrible, fiery fate.

Side by side with these rumours, and such irrational fear and behaviour, I noticed that a large number of young and middle-aged women, who came to seek my services as a sanusi, women from different parts of Soweto and from other townships in the Transvaal who did not know each other, were having dreams which had one astonishing thing in common. This made me realize that there was a sickness sweeping through the entire black community and that great danger lay ahead for the entire country in the very near future. The women were all dreaming of large crowds of people running and screaming, as if fleeing from something, with huge fires burning somewhere in the background and lighting up the sky.

Some of the women were dreaming of soldiers or policemen running with guns as if a battle was in progress. I began to receive more and more reports of such dreams of crowds, movement and hinted-at conflict of some sort as 1974 faded into 1975. Then one day a black newspaper carried a report of how a well known Soweto prophet named Lillian had foretold that trouble was coming to Soweto in 1976. This woman said she had seen in a dream how a great ball of fire appeared out of the west of Soweto and rolled through the township, setting fire to buildings and vehicles, and how she had seen hundreds of children running and shouting "in great anger" while others stumbled and fell to lie motionless in the street.

People scoffed at Lillian's words, and laughed when she said in the newspaper that God had told her to hang flags outside her home and so protect her house and those of her neighbours from the "great fire" she had seen in her vision. This woman's prophecy was to come shatteringly true on that bright and beautiful day of June 16, 1976 as fire, riot and death swept through Soweto, and oddly enough the rioting did start in the west of Soweto and spread in all directions.

The prophet Lillian had not been the only person in Soweto to foresee the Soweto riots in either dream or vision form. I had been shown this coming tragedy in several vivid dreams I had in the period 1973 to 1974; and then in 1975, while I was in the United States, I had the most vivid dream of all that showed me that South Africa would be engulfed by violence from 1976 to 1989, when this country as we know it will cease to exist as a military dictatorship takes over the reins of Government.

Two of the best sangomas in the group of healers and diviners of which I am the ritual leader, Mrs Mateilari Teka and Mrs Dorcas Danisa, were also shown the fiery disaster that was to overtake South Africa in 1976, 1986 and 1989. Mrs Danisa had her vision in 1975 just as I was preparing to go to America, and in the vision she saw the Virgin Mary holding a calendar in her hands and telling her that death and conflict were coming to South Africa and that when that happened she, Mrs Danisa, was to go out into the streets and try and save black children from getting killed. I, Credo Mutwa, was to assist her in my capacity as High Sanusi. It was because of this strange vision that on June 16, 1976 when the violence erupted in Soweto, Dorcas and I donned our best regalia and walked to Phefeni Station where the rioting was fiercest and tried to persuade school children to go home. We managed to persuade only ten frightened youngsters to leave the place of flame and violence, and then walked back home with despairing and exhausted hearts, our mission having failed.

Mrs Teka, who is an expert at what we call "cloud-divining"; that is, divining by studying the shapes of a cloud in the sky, found me standing at one of the front windows of my home staring at the scattered clouds that were drifting slowly across the face of the blue skies. She came to stand at my side, also staring at the sky, and long moments of silence went by before she said: "Father Mutwa, look at that cloud. That one over there".

"What do you see in it, child?" I asked her.

"There are little human figures in it, all of them seem to be running," she replied "That cloud worries me, Father".

"Why?" I asked, "what do your ancestral spirits tell you the cloud means?"

"There is a great conflict coming to our country, Father," replied the slender, dark-skinned Tswana girl. "Many of our people are going to die."

Mrs Mateilari Teka made her "cloud prophesy" on the second weekend of February, 1976 about a week after my return from the United States, exactly three months before the June riots erupted.

19

Deeds of Terror

About two years before the 1976 Soweto riots I witnessed, among other ominous things, a worrying increase in certain kinds of crime in our townships. They were bizarre, nauseating crimes that indicated to me there was something drastically wrong with the very soul of our people, that there was a definite illness sweeping through the entire black population of South Africa, an illness of the mind that forced people to commit deeds of unimaginable shamefulness and violence upon each other.

When a nation has been conquered by another nation it almost immediately goes into a state of something akin to shock which manifests itself in a number of clearly recognizable ways. Firstly the conquered nation casts about for a saviour or a number of hero-saviours who would take on the conquering nation single handed or at the head of a small band of loyal followers — and for a brief period restore the defeated nation's honour, in its own eyes at least. If hero-saviours fail to materialize then the defeated nation invents them, attributing to them superhuman strength, unshakable courage and godlike beauty. In short, the hero-saviours become the lone shining nucleus around which the defeated nation's pride, ideals and wishful thinking coalesces like the faintly glowing fragments of an exploded star in the deep, dark and deathly cold night of space.

But there comes a time when even mighty heroes must die, and after the nation's hero-saviour has died — usually a tragic and heroic death — the defeated nation starts to look reality in the face for the first time and shrinks before it as a terrified virgin shrinks before an advancing *"musutaraya"*[129] monster. The nation's spirit breaks and it disintegrates both morally, mentally and physically.

The defeated nation abandons its culture, values and religion and adopts those of the conquering nation wholesale, and this is always due to a deep-rooted feeling of resentment that culture and religion failed to help the nation in its hour of peril. The conquered nation becomes ashamed of its past and views its religion and culture with a feeling of repugnance and embarrassment.

After the Britons had been conquered by the Romans many forsook their traditional culture, way of life and religion and began adopting Roman ways and referring to themselves as Romans. They did this voluntarily through no coercion on the part of the Latins, and some even began to look with disgust upon the Druids and the native British religion and actually assisted the Romans in the destruction of Druidic sacred groves and other shrines. Exactly the same thing happened throughout Africa after its colonization by the European nations. Africans went out of their way to assist the colonists in the wholesale destruction of their native culture. In west Africa for example, "converts" to the Christian and Muslin faiths took axes and swords to the wooden statues of their native Gods, burned "Juju" and "Obeia" shrines and even killed wise-women and juju-priests like vermin, simply to impress the newly-arrived missionaries, who then rewarded them with cast-off cassocks, top-hats and military jackets in appreciation of what they had done.

In southern, eastern and central Africa, black traitors to their people's culture and religion encouraged English, Dutch and German missionaries to establish their mission stations and mission schools in areas once regarded sacred by generations of black people before the coming of the white man to Africa. The result of this is that many of the oldest mission schools and mission churches in Natal for example stand on ground once sacred to the Goddess Nomkumbulwana, the Sun-God Mvelinqangi and the dread Nkulunkulu, the Zulu God, the Father. In the west of Zululand there stands the great Qhudeni mountain — the Mountain of the Crowing Cock — which was once regarded as the abode of these three great Zulu deities. The mountain down which Mvelinqangi is said to have come to bring the great laws to the Zulu people in remote antiquity.

A traitorous Zulu convert led a group of missionaries to the foot of this sacred mountain and there, after some years, a Catholic mission school was established and named after this great mountain — Qhudeni. In order to hijack the name once long associated with traditional Zulu religion, the Catholics placed a weathercock — *Iqhude* in Zulu — on the steeple of the first church they built there. This cunning ploy was intended to invest the new mission school with the same aura of reverence the mountain had had in the eyes of thousands of Zulus for generations.

I have recently learned much to my surprise that when Christianity started spreading across the face of Europe, the early Christian monks did exactly the same as the later missionaries were to do in Africa in the 19th century . . . they established their greatest abbeys and churches upon the sites of ancient temples and stone-circles that had first been demolished by over-zealous converts to the new religion.

As the traditional culture and religion of the defeated people fade or go underground, as traditional values and practices disintegrate, so the moral structure of the nation begins to fall apart. Things such as promiscuity, excessive abuse of alcohol and habit forming drugs, as well as crime of all kinds, begin proliferating among the defeated people. The entire population takes the downward-sloping path to moral, spiritual and physical ruin.

The lifespans of the defeated people start to grow shorter. For example: extreme longevity was quite common among black people throughout southern Africa in the last century, and there was not a single village or kraal that could not boast one or two or even three people well past their hundredth year of life. Some of the people lived for so long they were no longer capable of swallowing the finest of liquid foods; and their flesh, especially that of their buttocks, began to peel off, creating terrible sores that were no longer capable of healing. Such people had to be put out of their misery in a form of euthanasia which, among the Zulus, consisted of taking the old person into a cattle-pen and then driving a large herd of cattle over him or her while he or she lay — heavily drugged — on a white cowhide.

Today black people count themselves lucky to see their seventieth year of life, so short has the black life expectancy become, especially in the urban areas. The moment that happens to the defeated people after the shortening of their lifespans, they become excessively violent first against members of their own race and later against members of the race that conquered them. This violence is due partly to fear, partly to stress and partly to a deep-rooted feeling of inferiority and chronic spiritual confinement within the four walls of an invisible prison. The conquered people start behaving exactly as rats behave in one ancient Zulu experiment looking into animal behaviour. In this experiment six rats were captured and imprisoned in a large clay pot with a clay lid. The pot was then carefully heated over a slow fire with a heavy stone over the lid. Fear and pain cause the large rodents to turn on each other, biting each other to death.

The defeated people are always under chronic, deadly stress often without being aware of it for generation after generation after their defeat. The defeated people become victim to all sorts of phobias and groundless beliefs and suspicions, most of them directed at their conquerors, and in this the black man of South Africa is no exception. For years now black people have entertained quite bizarre and utterly groundless beliefs about whites, which are all known to, and are exploited to the hilt by, subversive organizations such as the ANC.

There are crimes of extreme barbarity that very rarely get reported to the police in black townships, crimes so obscene that their victims become so utterly shocked and shattered that they totally refuse to report the matter, choosing rather to let a foul criminal go free rather than reveal their agony and degradation in court. One of these crimes is the rape of a man by another man, a sort of crime that suddenly increased in townships such as Thembisa in 1974.

When most black men have been subjected to this sort of unnatural attack they become filled with guilt and overwhelming shame and they become obsessed with a feeling that they are unclean and therefore no longer fit to live. It becomes much worse for them if they happen to be Christians, because then they become filled with the idea they are now men doomed to eternal damnation after death because they have become tainted with the "sin of sodom."

Such men are always brought to the traditional healers by their friends or relatives for purification, comforting and strengthening, and so are mothers who have been raped by their sons, sisters who have been raped by their brothers or daughters who have been indecently assaulted or raped by their fathers. Such crimes were very rare in the townships, but in the years 1973 and 1974 there was a sudden and alarming increase in these crimes, and in one weekend alone I found myself attending to six victims of indecent assault.

Some months before the outbreak of the Soweto riots in 1976 another greatly disturbing thing appeared that turned out to be but a foretaste of much worse to come. School children became more and more inclined to take the law into their own hands and to mete out rough and often deadly justice to thugs who assaulted pupils or teachers in school. On one occasion a mob of school children murdered a criminal who had beaten up a female schoolteacher and robbed her of her handbag.

No thinking person can deny that the black people in South Africa have been spiritually ill for years and that their illness is going from bad to worse; and no one can deny that the cause of their illness has been long decades of degradation and repression. Our people are not only ill but they are also violently, bitterly angry, and it is this long pent-up rage that is now exploding outwards like a fiery nova and manifesting itself in all manner of atrocious and murderous deeds. Deeds such as a man attacking another man in a latrine, pummelling him with fists and then raping him before jumping over a fence like a midnight ape and running away and deeds such as cold-bloodily binding a screaming woman hand and foot and then burning her alive with a tractor tyre.

The burning of people alive in the townships is one of the most barbaric things that is occurring in our country. But these rage-maddened people do much more than just burn the people to death. First they batter them with rocks, stab them with knives and then burn them. And afterwards they crowd around the burning, writhing corpse and deliberately inhale the fumes of the burning flesh. They can even go to the extent of tearing bits of charred flesh from the dead body and eating them. And when you see such a sight, as I have seen it several times, your mind totally refuses to believe what your eyes are seeing, so bizarre, so horrible and so unearthly is the spectacle.

I am a man who has seen much in his life, a man who has travelled far. I was born and I grew up in a part of Natal that was a scene of sporadic faction fighting for decades, and from early childhood I grew accustomed to the sight of death, death in its most horrid and most violent form. I have seen death in other parts of Africa too: whole kraals and villages wiped clean of human life only the grey bodies of dead men and women lay horribly swollen and decaying in the hot African sun. I have seen all this and much more, but the sights that I have seen in our townships in the last ten years or so have left me shaken, shaken all the more because I know exactly why they happened.

If I was a person of importance in South Africa, which I am not, and if my word carried any weight, which it does not, I would appeal to the powers-that-be to treat our people with mercy and to make sure that all the suffering and the hardship that accompanied apartheid becomes a thing of the past. It is no good to be told there there is a reform process going on in South Africa. We must *feel* that things are changing, we must *experience* change, everyone of us, but at this moment we feel nothing and experience nothing.

All we feel is that our country is heading for hell, that the townships have become foul unlivable dens of death, arson and intimidation and that most parents are now faced with no other choice than to get their children out of the townships as quickly as possible. All we see in the townships are corrupt officials and the great heaps of refuse that are accumulating on street corners because the refuse collecting vehicles have either been destroyed or that their drivers have become so brutally intimidated that they can no longer carry out their duties.

The fear under which we have lived in the black townships has multiplied a thousand-fold in the last three years. Today we no longer fear only the street-gang or the night-skulking criminal, but we fear the groups of wild-eyed and bloody-handed zealots who kill and mutilate for different political "causes."

Today when you watch your children leaving your house to go to school, you do not know which of them will fail to return, killed by either the so-called "comrades" or by some trigger-happy policeman.

20

A Matter of Communication

The biggest cause of the bloody trouble South Africa is in, is that neither now nor in the past has there been any full, frank and in-depth communication between the black man and the white man. Ever since the first years that the white man became master and the black man the cringing servant, the black man has carefully and deliberately kept a vital part of himself unknown to the white man.

The aim of this being, firstly, to keep the white man in the dark about his true feelings, thoughts and intentions and so to retain a psychological advantage over him. Secondly, to shield those things the black man believes in; thus preventing the white man from knowing the full truth and using it against the black man in the future.

For centuries now blacks have been taught that: "When an enemy invades your country, crushes you in battle and makes slaves of you, you must yield to him and become his slaves quietly. This you must do in order to survive the angry night of enslavement, to survive until one day you are strong enough to rid your country of the invader. But remember, you must never allow the enemy to possess your innermost minds because should the enemy achieve this, so then you will be his dogs forever more.

"Learn from your enemy, but never allow him to learn anything from you. Flatter him, play upon his arrogance as a maiden plays upon a harp. Bemoan and degrade yourselves in his eyes, play stupid just as the jackal, caught in the paws of an angry lion, hangs out its tongue and plays dead. Remember, the gods of time always favour the invaded and the vanquished . . . ."

In the past, this strange philosophy has served defeated tribes well, enabling them to survive where stiff-necked and proud nations would perish. Thus, when the white man came to Africa and conquered tens of thousands of our people, they immediately activated this time-tried survival system of allowing the conqueror to possess and abuse their bodies, but never to gain possession of their minds. In South Africa especially, the white man has boasted many times that he understands the black man and has studied him well, when all that he has studied is the smoke-screen behind which the black man has for years carefully hidden his true self.

One of the most effective tricks that the African employs upon those who have conquered him is to quickly adopt the habits, laws, attire and customs of the conqueror-nation and even go to the extent of exaggerating them slightly. All this being part of the chameleon like survival camouflage whose idea is that no man will ever harm anything that resembles him outwardly, and that in order to avoid extermination at the hands of your conqueror you must turn yourself into a slightly exaggerated mirror-image of him; thus fooling him into thinking that he has so thoroughly intimidated you and that his domination over you is now so complete that you are glad to imitate his ways.

The black in South Africa has succeeded so well in this form of deception that he has been able to catch the white man by surprise time and again in many ways. He has been able, for example, to openly plan acts of violence without the white man knowing what is afoot until too late, and nothing illustrates this more vividly, than the 1976 Soweto riots.

Just before the tragedy took place there were already people who knew that there was going to be trouble of a major kind in Soweto. All the danger signs were already up, visible to all observant black people in the vast township complex, but completely unseen by the police and by officials of the West Rand Administration Board. Two white men stumbled upon the truth by sheer accident, because they happened to be working close to the black people in Soweto. One of them a television film producer and the other a man named Mr Melville Edelstein.[130] Mr Edelstein's duty in Soweto was to give assistance to black youths who were in difficulties with obtaining their identity papers.

I remember the day when Mr Edelstein came to visit me at the traditional museum I had built in Soweto. He asked me what the purpose of all the buildings he saw around him was, and when I told him that it was a cultural exercise designed to bring the black man closer to his roots, he asked: "Do you think it will do any good? I think you are too late by ten years, my friend." He went on to tell me that he had felt an ugly tension mounting in Soweto since the beginning of 1975 and that he was sure there was going to be some kind of explosion in the township complex.

That was in May, 1975, a cold and cloudless afternoon, and when the dark-haired and bespectacled white man left our kraal museum I did not realize that the next time I would see him would be as a horribly mutilated corpse lying some distance away from his burnt out and still smoldering office. That hellish day will forever be engraved in my memory in images of blood, fire and smoke, Wednesday June 16, 1976. This gentle Jew had been brutally stoned to death and then the entire contents of a rubbish bin had been emptied over his head — the work of pro-PLO activists who lurk inside the membership of the ANC.

The other white man, the film-producer free-lancing for the SABC, got short shrift from one of his superiors when he tried to take a warning about the coming disaster to that august organization of purblind ostriches with their heads firmly buried in the sands of history and ignorance. He was, so he said afterwards to a newspaper-reporter, "literally kicked out of the office."

South Africa is very cruel to her prophets — black and white. She allows them the painful luxury of having their homes burnt, of being stoned or burnt to death and of being booted out of SABC offices. Truly, are prophets without honour in the lands of their birth?

Few white South Africans pay any close attention to their servants. Some "madams" in the posh white suburbs of Johannesburg cannot even tell you what their maid's surname is. Most of this is the servant's own deliberate doing, because black houseservants are past masters and past mistresses of melting into the background, visible yet unseen, quiet but bitterly articulate, and drawing as little attention to themselves as possible. They do this by imitating their employers as much as possible, in attire, mannerisms and sometimes even in accent, but some of them tend to fall into the trap of imitating their employer's worst characteristics such as snobbishness and arrogance — especially towards fellow black people.

The employer is usually the last person to learn about the grievances and the true feelings of his servants, because he is the very last person on earth to whom they speak about such things. Any employer who ever tells you that he or she knows what his or her servants like or dislike, what they believe in or do not believe in, is merely indulging in gross self-deception.

I have visited many farms, firms and other places where black people are employed in large numbers and found that the employer prides himself in being good to his "boys" or "girls" and yet I find the servant's view of this man is anything but that which he entertains about himself. This habit of never revealing the truth about themselves to their employers has on many occasions brought disaster crashing upon the servant's head as the following little incident I witnessed while working as a house-servant will show you.

There were four of us in the large house, there was old Majola the gardener, there was me the cook, Eliza the "nanny" and Tryphina, a Swazi woman of the royal Dlamini clan,[131] the house-cleaner. One day, one of our employer's fox-terriers, a fierce but lovely little beast named Scandal, lived up to her name by leaving a smelly present to all and sundry upon one of the polished steps that led up to the verandah of the big house. Our employer's wife saw this and ordered Tryphina to "remove the dog-turd from the stoep." To her surprise the black woman, who had worked for this household for five loyal years ignored her employer's command. Then our employer's daughter walked up to Tryphina and ordered her to remove the mess from the stoep immediately. Tryphina burst into hysterical tears, ran to her room, packed her things and left her job . . . leaving an astonished "madam" behind her.

The white family put the whole thing down to "these ungrateful god-damned natives." But we three remaining blacks knew the truth, the sad, tragic African truth that we did not reveal to our employer and her family. Tryphina had been childless for years and had already suffered the disintegration of two marriages as a result. Her third husband brought her to me and I had successfully identified the cause of her infertility as a deep-rooted fear of all men, caused by having been raped as a child by her elder brother.

I had successfully cured Tryphina of her fear of being penetrated by a male organ and she had become pregnant some two months later much to the delight of her Mukaranga[132] husband. When Scandal started the trouble by excreting on the stoep, Tryphina was already two months pregnant and as is the case with all pregnant women throughout Africa, she was ruled by many taboos and was forbidden from walking over or even touching things such as the dung of a dog or a cat for example, just as she was forbidden to eat certain foods according to our ancient laws. Tryphina had chosen rather to lose a job she had held for five years, than defile her unborn baby and so expose herself to the agonies of a possible miscarriage . . . .

That he has for years denied the white man access to his innermost beliefs, fears and thoughts, has many times saved the black man both as an individual or as a people from really serious trouble. It has also, however, had the effect of plunging him into much suffering as well. I could give you well over a hundred examples of how black men managed to escape trouble by relying on the white man's lack of knowledge about black ways and customs and the way the black man thinks.

One day I was invited by a friend of mine, the late Justice JF Ludorf[133] of Johannesburg, to come to the Supreme Court and listen as he tried cases — an invitation I gladly accepted.

Justice Ludorf told me that he had come very close to hanging a completely innocent man, because his knowledge of black customs and traditions was so poor. He said the man, a young Zulu, had been brought before him charged with the brutal killing of his father, and as the trial progressed he had noticed the accused was unusually relaxed as evidence sure to send him to the gallows was piled up against him. He had been arrested while sitting on a bench outside the shack in which his father's body lay. The axe which had been used in the murder was found cradled in his hands.

He had confessed to everything, saying how he had hated his father for years and had wanted to see him dead for a long time. He said his father had struck him for no reason as he entered the shack, and he then hacked his father down with the axe.

"The young man was relaxed, too relaxed, Credo," said the judge, "and he was so calm right through the trial that I began to suspect all was not as it should be. I became more suspicious when the man started demanding I pass the death sentence upon him, saying he knew and we all knew he was guilty and I was wasting time.

"I postponed sentencing the young bugger and ordered a more thorough investigation, and the facts were at last revealed. The young man had returned home from Johannesburg and found, to his horror, his mother had just murdered his father, and he had done the traditional thing of chivalrously taking the blame in an effort to save his mother. It was this case that made me interested in the book you wrote and what you have to say about your people's traditions in it. I feel you should write more books on this subject, don't you?"

The book that the judge was referring to was my first book, *Indaba My Children*, [134] published in 1964, a book that I had hoped would be the first of a series of books that would have helped to bridge the wide gulf between black and white in South Africa and that would have also, perhaps, contributed something towards averting the awesome catastrophe I was certain would overtake this country.

One of the most terrible things that can happen to a person gifted with a modicum of second sight is to see each one of the prophesies that you made years and years ago come horribly true; and this has been the case with me, and truly my life is no longer worth living.

21

Superstition and Intimidation

The white man knows so little about the black man in South Africa, and as a result the black man has been able to openly do many things that he would have done in secret had the opposite been the case. Again and again he has been able to get away with many ugly things he would not otherwise have escaped with.

For example, black radicals intimidate people openly almost hourly in the townships. Not only do they intimidate but they also invite their terrified victims to go and complain to the police, secure in the knowledge that the police would not know what the victim was babbling about and would refuse to believe him and throw him out of the police station.

Some weeks before my home was attacked in 1976 by a mob, anonymous people would make a habit of throwing old horseshoes into my yard. This is one of the many methods of savage intimidation employed by the radicals, methods based upon black traditional beliefs and superstitions. White people regard horseshoes as symbols of good luck, but to black people a horseshoe is a symbol of ghosts and of death in its most violent form. If I throw horseshoes into the yard of your home I am threatening you with a death of extreme violence, a death after which your ghost will haunt the place where you died for all eternity. Had I tried to report this to the police, who were unfamiliar with black superstitions they would have had me certified or sent me packing.

After the 1976 Soweto riots, a number of politically inspired murders took place in Soweto and other townships, murders in which the ANC was implicated. The victims of these murders were either policemen or former members of the ANC. All these murders had one thing in common, the VICTIMS WERE ALL MURDERED IN THEIR HOMES.

Now, according to tradition killing, a person in his or her home is designed to fill his or her family, friends and neighbours, with a cold and cloying terror. It is in fact a form of brutal mass-intimidation similar to the burning of a human being alive with a car tyre. The ANC has employed this form of terrorization with great effect in South Africa in the last twelve years.

There was a man named "Mbatha"; of Dube township in Soweto who was shot down one night by an ANC assassin in front of his only son. Now, the killing of a parent in front of a child or children is yet another form of terrorization on a massive scale, and in old Africa, members of secret societies that practiced evil, murdered the parents in order to gain possession of the children. By killing the parent in front of his or her children the secret society was showing those children that it possessed greater power over them than their slaughtered parent or parents ever had and they were therefore at its mercy and must be prepared to obey all commands in future.

I have every reason to believe that just as the ancient secret societies killed parents in order to gain possession of those children so do modern terrorist organizations in Africa, including the ANC.

Like ancient evil secret societies modern African terrorist organizations practice large-scale kidnappings of people as an effective means of demonstrating their power. In old Africa few things were more feared than the person who specialized in catching people alive and carrying them off to some mysterious destination for mysterious purposes. In those days being captured was seen as the "deepest disgrace" that could befall any person anywhere, and it was the one thing guaranteed to break the spirit of any person, male or female, which is why Zulus and other tribes still have a custom known as "Ukuthwala Intombi" which means "to carry off the maiden," a custom used to break the spirit of arrogant maidens who still persisted on refusing to say yes to a young man's wooing even after the young man has wooed the girl for the required period.

The young man would then acquire the services of a professional kidnapper of whom there were many in those days and this cunning man would waylay the girl, seize her, carry her off to her wooer's kraal, dump her there and then collect his fee. The love-struck young man would quickly impregnate the girl and then send messengers to the girl's father, telling him where his daughter was and offering to pay the required bride-price for her . . . .

22

The Power Behind the Numbers . . . a Prediction

If you were ever to write down all the dates in which events of great and violent importance took place, not only in southern Africa but also in other parts of Africa, in the last thirty-five years or so you will find, on carefully studying that list, that almost all those dates will have something in common. You will find much to your surprise that nearly all major events in Africa have not happened at random but rather have followed a definite and rather disquieting pattern, and that if you are familiar with the strange facts behind this pattern you will be able to predict, with remarkable accuracy, when, in the course of which year, during which month or months and even on what day other momentous events involving Africa and her people will occur.

For example, I wish to make this prediction: Unless the present violence in South Africa is ended immediately, it will go from bad to worse and South Africa as we know it, will have either ceased to exist by the year 1989, or will be under a ruthless military dictatorship. Tens of thousands of black people will be incarcerated in concentration camps and protected villages and several millions will have perished. I say that unless reason and moderation prevail, the year 1989 will become the most violent and most dangerous year in our country's history. Exactly why do I make this prediction and why am I so sure that it will come to pass?

The Nationalist Government came to power in South Africa in

the year 1948, and in the year 1949 bloody riots broke out in the city of Durban between the Zulus and the Indians. The years 1953 and 1956 as well as 1959 saw the coming and escalation of political violence in South Africa. The year 1959 had special significance for the Rhodesians as well in that it marked the beginning of the downfall of the Central African Federation,[135] for it was in that year that there began widespread rioting in Southern Rhodesia,[136] Northern Rhodesia[137] and Nyasaland.[138] This led to the rise of black leaders such as Joshua Nkomo,[139] Kenneth Kaunda[140] and Dr Hastings Banda[141] and the eventual disintegration of Sir Roy Welensky's[142] federation of Northern and Southern Rhodesia and the Nyasaland Protectorate.

The year 1960 was an extremely tragic one for South Africa, because it was in that year the Sharpeville shootings took place — on March 21. In 1963 South Africa was under a State of Emergency[143] and I want you to know that it is by no means a coincidence that our country is again under a State of Emergency.

In 1966 the South African security police were extremely active and young black militants were already beginning to leave South Africa, some to go to Ghana, which was then the refuge of black exiles from southern Africa. Others were sent to Eastern Bloc and other communist countries for military training under the aegis of the ANC.

In 1969 there was tension and sporadic violence and intimidation in South Africa while in Mr Ian Smith's[144] Rhodesia, the first incursions by armed black guerrilla groups began, causing much contemptuous laughter among the white Rhodesians.

These minor incursions always ended in death or arrest for the terrorists and the Rhodesians were sure that such incursions would soon cease, because the "terrs" of that time appeared to have no stomach for a real fight and either gave in easily or were tracked down and destroyed. But time was to prove the Rhodesians fatally wrong . . . .

The year 1973 saw the coming of "black power"[145] to South Africa when thousands of young black intellectuals started talking about a thing they called "negritude,"[146] and this thing was to develop into the philosophy of "black consciousness,"[147] which was the moving philosophy behind the Soweto Riots of 1976 — just as it is the force behind the present unrest.

The world knows what happened in South Africa in 1976; but

it may interest you to know that June 16 was a Wednesday, a day which has played an extremely sinister part in the history of southern Africa in the last thirty years or more.

The year 1979 brought more tension and more drama to South Africa. There were incidents of unrest in places such as Soweto, and in one particularly horrible incident a Soweto school principal lost his wife and children when his home was petrol-bombed by a rioting mob.

But the most revealing incident by far in 1979 took place not in South Africa, but rather in Tanzania and Uganda when President Julius Nyerere,[148] who for years had endured provocation and virulent insult from the fat and strutting Ugandan Dictator Idi Amin,[149] suddenly unleashed the full fury of his country's army upon Uganda. He routed not only the ill-disciplined Ugandan army, but also a force of Libyans sent to assist the black buffoon by fellow madman Colonel Muammar al-Qaddafi of Libya, and Nyerere sent Amin fleeing for his tyrannical life.

If you take, for example, the date of the Sharpeville shootings, (March 21, 1960) and the date of the Soweto Riots, (June, 16 1976) you shall find on carefully studying them that they both have one important thing in common, namely that the number three plays a very prominent part. I want to tell you here and now that this is not at all an accident, nor is it a coincidence. Even before the 1976 tragedy there was a day in the month of June which was celebrated as a holiday by black political activists and supporters of the ANC, and that day is known as Freedom Day and it falls on June, 26. It marks the drawing up and signing of the Freedom Charter[150] of the ANC in the stinking slum-land known as Kliptown just outside Soweto.

The Freedom Charter was signed in 1956 and this shows that long before 1976, the month of June was regarded as an important month by followers of the ANC, otherwise why did they choose to put this important day in this particular month?

Anyone who has studied African culture and history in depth knows that all the black tribes and nations throughout Africa possessed knowledge of the calendar for hundreds if not thousands of years and that all tribes have a traditional name for each one of the months of the year, each month being about twenty-eight days long — and not thirty or thirty-one days.

Now the blacks, with their bubbling sense of humour, have given each month a very revealing and extremely humurous name. For instance June is known by the Tswana people as *Seetebosigo,* which means the *"do-not-visit-by-night-month"* and it is so named because June is the coldest month of the year in this part of Africa. It is the month where black people bring out *all the* blankets they own and cover themselves thickly so that a visiting friend who decides to spend the night will find his or her host and hostess will have no blanket to spare.

In the Zulu language the month January is known as *Undasa,* which means "the-big-stomach-month." During this month Zulus had plenty of maize, milk and sorghum to eat.

They also gave names to each year that went by; but unlike the months, whose names never changed, the years were given names only according to major events that took place. For example: 1918 is known by the Zulus as *"Unyaka Wembo"* or *"the-great-fever-year"* in recollection of the great influenza epidemic that swept the whole world.

Christians count their years from the birth of Jesus Christ, Israelis count theirs from the deliverance of Israel from Egyptian captivity by the prophet Moses, while Muslims count their years from the Hegira — Muhammad's flight from Mecca to Medina. So, according to which event did the Africans count their years? The answer is very simple, each tribe counted its years from the year of its founding, thus the Zulu people counted their years from the year of the founding of the Zulu tribe by King Zulu[151] some 530 years ago. If a tribe broke away from another tribe it immediately started counting its years from the year of breaking away, and just as is the case with western nations, which sometimes celebrate the date of their founding, so it was with African tribes who used to celebrate the year of their founding after every fifty years with feasting and dancing as well as with solemn religious rituals.

Our people counted their years in groups of ten, and at the end of each decade special ceremonies and celebrations were held and oracles of all kinds were consulted to find out what the next ten years held in store. The third, sixth and ninth year of every decade were regarded as years in which the tribe could undertake major military ventures FOR A GOOD CAUSE with a great chance of success.

Europeans, as well as Asians, believe in lucky and unlucky days, in lucky and unlucky animals, in lucky and unlucky objects, charms and substances as well as in lucky and unlucky numbers. And so do the African tribes, and one of the numbers our people regard as being lucky is the number three.

If a tribe has been attacked or otherwise humiliated by another tribe it must only retaliate when the day, month and year is right for it to do so, and this is why you always find that there are those months in the year when faction-killings increase suddenly. If you study this particular phenomenon closely you will find that these killings become worse in the months of March, June, September and December — the third, sixth, ninth and twelfth months of the year.

When the month of June 1986 drew to a close, two Johannesburg Sunday newspapers, the Sunday Times and The Sunday Star — both dated June, 29 — carried reports of a faction-war that had broken out in Zululand near the infamous town of Umsinga. This resulted in the flight, from his farm, of Mr Sipho Mchunu who had retired from the Juluka pop-group he and Mr Clegg had founded. It is reported that the faction-war was fought over Mchunu's farm and he had been forced to flee into the bush to escape the killings.

This young Zulu singer did a very unusual thing after retiring. He used some of his money to build a school for Zulu children in his district in order to bring education to this depressed, hunger-haunted and war-town area of KwaZulu. Then his own people turned on him and forced him to flee for his life. Africa always rejects and destroys those of her sons and daughters who bring light to her timeless valleys; Africa is a cruel mother who often devours her offspring.

Now, I want you to imagine a black rabble-rouser and trouble-maker, who wants to make a name for himself and his organization. This trouble-maker is a highly educated, cynical and modern person, who regards himself as being free of the beliefs and superstitions of his tribe. Furthermore this black self-deluding upstart considers himself a communist out to save "the exploited black masses" from the chains of capitalism. He then gathers around him a following of like-minded toadies and lickspittles who share his dream of a communist Azania, which, so they hope, would soon rise phoenix-like from the ashes of a destroyed South Africa.

This man and his friends are all intellectuals with the typical African intellectual's aversion to perishing in the "revolutionary struggle" they so passionately ferment. So like all true cowards they start looking around for cannon-fodder, and they find it by the thousands among the youth of the township in which they dwell. It is here that they encounter their first serious problem. Many of these youths are bound by the beliefs of their forbears and will undertake no violent action, for love, Karl Marx, or money unless the day is a lucky one or the month is one in which activities such as they are planning are assured of success.

When the planned violence has started and some of this would be liberator's followers perish in the "struggle" he, who claims to be free of superstition and who claims to frown upon black culture and customs as irrelevant nonsense, will nevertheless dig deep into that culture and those customs in order to deify the dead followers and so give the deluded rabble gods to look up to, in order to keep them firmly united and also to give some kind of religious aura to their many deeds of violence and rapine.

This is why you see many odd things done at the funerals of unrest victims and leading black activists who died in detention, odd things which will be meaningless to you unless you are versed in the mysteries of black religion and tradition.

For instance, when the late Robert Sobukwe[152] and Steve Biko were buried, the coffins were carried to the cemetery not in modern hearses but in donkey carts. This being a revival of the ancient African custom in which the body of a dead hero, god-king or even a sanusi was always borne to the graveyard in an ox-drawn sled or ox-drawn travois. By being taken to the graveyard in this way Sobikwe and Biko were actually being publicly deified . . . by a cynical organization whose aim is not only to destroy black religion and culture once it comes to power in South Africa but also to take the priests and priestesses of that religion — the inyangas, sanusis and sangomas and throw them into "re-education centres," shoot them or "necklace" them.

There is another custom seen at the funerals of political activists in South African black townships. This is the custom of carrying the dead person's coffin shoulder-high as it is borne to the graveyard. This practice is again an ancient custom in which the body of a great warrior, who had died for a good cause, was carried on his or her shield (we had female warriors aplenty in those days, for there was no sex discrimination in Africa) to the place of burial by fellow warriors. By doing so the warriors were taking a solemn oath not to stop fighting until they had all died exactly as the dead friend they were burying had died.

Yet another and rather bizzarre custom seen at funerals, is that of the mourners shouting at the coffin and beating it with sticks and pummelling it with fists, working themselves into a blazing rage in the process. This custom is an ancient Basutho warrior-custom that was still being practised in the the townships before it was taken over by political activists. Here activists attack the dead man's coffin with sticks and beat it almost to splinters before it is lowered into the grave. While beating the coffin, they shout friendly insults at the dead body — calling it a coward who had died in order to escape the fighting. They then promise that ten of the enemy would die in revenge.

In the past, such weird ceremonies had the aim of keeping the tribe united, and its rage at fever-heat during times of inter-tribal war. They also placed the dead person in the memories of the living as a god or ancestral spirit. These customs have now been adopted by various black political organizations for exactly the same reasons.

A more absurd belief that has for over fifty years circulated in black communities is that the white man is greatly troubled by the increasing number of black people in South Africa. It is believed that in order to keep black numbers down successive South African governments have deliberately allowed violent crime to flourish in the townships. It is also believed that this is in order to bring about the deaths of as many people as possible at the hands of criminals, which is why police in the townships rarely catch murderers who have killed blacks but easily catch those black criminals who have murdered whites in the cities. There are also beliefs that the white man often deliberately engineers train and bus accidents in which blacks die in large numbers.

These weird beliefs may seem silly to you but they are held by tens of thousands of blacks throughout South Africa and were exploited in pamphlets distributed by the ANC in 1976 to fan the flames of violence. These beliefs have also been exploited by the use of deliberately disseminated word-of-mouth rumours, over the last five years, to further destroy the already shaky confidence that our people have in the Government, the police and the judiciary throughout South Africa. This is why today we see more and more black people taking the law into their own hands, and why kangaroo courts, which try people and sentence them — sometimes to death

— are now part and parcel of everyday life in nearly all major black townships throughout South Africa.

In parts of Soweto such as Meadowlands, Diepkloof, Chiawelo and Zola, a wife troubled by her drunken husband who beats her up, refuses to support her and her children choosing rather to spend his meagre earnings on liquor and cheap prostitutes, no longer bothers to go and seek help in the offices of the Black Affairs Commissioner in Market Street, Johannesburg, but rather she wraps a shawl around her shoulders and goes in search of the chief commissioner of the local "comrades"[153] group. Justice will be swift, painful and effective. The comrades will invade the man's home, seize him and quickly bind him hand and foot with lengths of copper-wire, and then he will be told by the leading comrade that he is accused of being an enemy of the people who ill-treats "the comrade his wife" and that "the people's court" has sentenced him to receive sixteen lashes with a length of electrical cord or a sjambok made out of a motorcar's fanbelt. The thrashing will be long and howlingly painful and then the husband is warned that he will face a rather fiery demise unless he mends his ways — the comrades place a tyre, "necklace," around his neck for a few moments. Needless to say the wretched man recovers with a vengeance and becomes one of the best fathers in Soweto . . . .

I say the black people in Africa have very strange beliefs and customs that the radical groups exploit to the fullest. The year 1989 could have tragic consequences for South Africa and her people.

23

The Spread of Communism in South Africa

We, the people of South Africa regardless of race, colour or creed, are among the cruellest nations on earth. We idolize force and we worship mindless authority, and shamelessly kowtow to the bludgeoning *thug,* the sneak *thief* and the bloody-handed *murderer.* We not only bow down before these ugly symbols of extraordinary evil, but we go out of our way to emulate them — placing them upon the highest pedestal in the halls of our minds.

We are a vicious, bloodthirsty people and our womenfolk are even more so. Anyone who has seen South African women of all races cheering and screaming with almost orgasmic joy at the obscene spectacle of two boxers or wrestlers battering each other to unconsciousness in the blood-splattered ring, knows damn well what I am talking about.

Anyone who has ever worked, as I once worked, in a yard belonging to the Society for the Prevention of Cruelty to Animals (SPCA) and seen scores of sad-eyed kittens, dogs and other animals, cruelly abandoned yearly by their white owners, which eventually have to be given the fatal injection and destroyed because no home can be found, will also know just what I am talking about. Anyone who has ever walked through a typical modern black township and seen the sight of horses, dogs and cats, thin and emaciated with dull, death-haunted eyes being subjected to mutilation and other forms of cold-blooded cruelty by black adults and children will know what I am angry about.

And have you ever sat, as I have done many times, in the "charge office" of South African Police stations and seen the long line of victims of savage assault, women with torn and bloody dresses, men with heads and chests astream with blood, victims of rape, indecent assault, "common assault" and other forms of man's inhumanity to fellow human beings, parading like an unending nightmare before the cold and uncaring eyes of policemen long hardened by such revolting sights?

Have you ever sat, as I have done many times, in the reception areas of South African hospitals, such as Baragwanath Hospital to the south of Johannesburg, and seen ambulance after ambulance and taxi after taxi, bring in blood-covered howling, screaming and even dying horrors, which only a few hours before were living and thinking human beings . . . before they met the *mugger, the rapist, the maniac and the jealous lover?*

We, the people of South Africa, are fond of contact sports such as soccer and rugby; we burn our throats out cheering the Springboks at Ellis Park Stadium in Johannesburg and howl like huge wolf-packs, and even fly at each other's throats like rabid wolves, when the Kaizer Chiefs[154] are in action under the flood-lights of the Orlando Soccer Stadium in Soweto.

We deem ourselves to be a sophisticated and sport-loving nation, but our love for these particular sports reveals the blazing streak of demonic cruelty that quivers within our minds. We want to be loved by the outside world, but we are capable of loving nobody. We want to be understood and yet ourselves understand nothing and no one, and daily we proclaim ourselves Christians, but our deeds proclaim us to be more closely related to those Romans who fed early Christians to lions in Rome's arenas, than to the humble, fearless and enlightened followers of Christ of those bygone years.

In South Africa it is quite common for a parent to slaughter his or her children before committing suicide. South Africa has one the highest rate of executions in the western world, one of the highest divorce rates in the world as well as a prison population of such size it would have made Nikita Khrushchev[155] and Joseph Stalin[156] green with communistic envy. And furthermore this country boasts one of the highest road-accident rates on earth and the highest rate of heart attacks known to modern man.

There is definitely something wrong with South Africa. There is something wrong with this country not only physically but also spiritually; and the shining stars of fate decree one end and one end only for a country such as this unless it mends its ways now. A fate similar to that which overtook Rome, Babylon and Sumeria.

We the people of South Africa, regardless of race, colour or creed, stand guilty of many sins before the shining judgement seat of the Most High. We stand guilty of many dark sins for which we should ask God's forgiveness.

But by far the greatest sin that we are all guilty of is our lack of feeling and our lack of understanding for each other. For well over three hundred weary years we have been living together in one country like shipwrecked sailors bundled together by a cruel fate in one leaky little boat. During all that time we have never made any serious efforts to know each other, respect each other's feelings, nor to communicate with each other fully and frankly across the slowly widening racial and colour barriers.

We have lived together in this land with masks of deceit covering our real faces and have made a fetish out of our superficial differences disregarding the many things that we have in common and which prove us to be the true offspring of the All-Highest. For well over three centuries we have allowed our view of each other to be coloured by hatred and prejudice, to be blinkered by ignorance and dimmed by the glaucoma of fantasy and utter falsehood. We have sinned greatly before the Almighty, and now throughout the length and breadth of this country we are beginning to pay in flame, blood and tears.

One of the strangest and most revealing things happening in Africa these days is that the communists, whom we are told are bent on world-domination, and whom we are told are trying to enslave Africa and seize the Cape sea route — thus denying the West, Africa's strategic minerals as well as Middle Eastern oil — are leaving alone the many weak nations in Africa they could crush with ease. Instead they are concentrating all their energies upon the destruction of South Africa. And we, the benighted denizens of this land have never once asked ourselves why this is so — save for the childish belief that our minerals and the Cape sea route are what the communists have their sights set on.

There are countries in Africa much bigger, with more people and that are more rich or potentially rich in mineral resources than South Africa is. For example: Zaire is much bigger than South Africa and possesses tremendous and as yet unexploited mineral wealth and has more people of different tribes and races than is the case with South Africa. It is ruled by a dictatorial megalomaniac named Mobutu Sese Seko,[157] who sees himself as something of a god and who is today regarded as the wealthiest black man in the world — because of having dabbled in bribery and corruption for many years.

If the communist warlords in Moscow, Havana or Peking wanted to seize Zaire they could do it overnight, but they show no signs of such thoughts. Nigeria is another case in point; this country is the most populated country in Africa and it occupies a highly-strategic position, tucked under the armpit of the African continent. Anyone who has ever worked in that country will tell you that it is inhabited by more people of different races than South Africa is and is cursed with interracial tensions and intertribal animosities even more than in our country. It is richer in mineral resources than South Africa could ever hope to be. Nigeria has vast untapped gold deposits, she is a member of the OPEC cartel of oil-producing nations and since the remotest of remote times, parts of this country have been scenes of prehistoric mining activities.

For decades, Nigeria has been ruled by a succession of corrupt governments some military and some civilian. Coup has followed disgraceful coup and the impression one gets is of a country both top-heavy and unwieldy as well as inherently unstable. Why then are the communists not seizing this golden prize, this ripe apple? If they did they would inflict more damage to European interests than they could if they seized South Africa and could still be in a position to interfere with western world trade routes in the Atlantic.

Why then are the communists concentrating their efforts firstly upon South Africa, when there are countries in Africa just as strategically positioned by fate they could seize with little trouble? And here is an amazing thought that has just occurred to me: Even those African countries that fell to the communists in the last twenty years or so, countries such as Mozambique, Angola and Zimbabwe, tumbled into the communist lap more by design than by accident.

In other words when the angry black nationalists of those countries started looking around for weapons with which to fight the ruling whites in earnest, the communists just happened to be the only people ready and willing to supply the nationalists with those weapons, with the result that the Africans became bound to the communists by bonds of gratitude thereafter and went through the motions, out of gratitude and nothing more, of moving into the communist orbit.

Since time immemorial, Africans have held the belief that: "He who gives me a spear to kill the rogue elephant and so save my village is a brother who I must follow to the day of my death." In ancient times if a tribe was under attack by another tribe and you appeared out of somewhere with weapons and armed the tribe under attack and thus enabled it to defeat its attackers, the tribe you had helped would thereafter willingly do anything you asked, even to the extent of sinking its identity and merging with your tribe and becoming one with it. Scores of tribes were absorbed this way by other tribes in southern Africa.

So then why are the communists concentrating their efforts upon South Africa when there happen to be easier targets elsewhere? Why would anyone waste time and energy in trying to subdue and chain a giant when there are pygmies living with that giant, pygmies he could conquer with ease and gain much more than he would by enslaving the giant? You would do that seemingly illogical thing only if you knew that the giant, though of wild and utterly fearsome aspect, is really a pathetically weak creature suffering from defects that would enable you to subdue him much faster than you would the pygmies. Defects such as poor eyesight, sore muscles, cracked ribs and weak kidneys . . . and a running stomach.

South Africa, on the surface, is the most militarily and economically powerful country in Africa and it has been proudly and repeatedly claimed by her military officers and politicians that her armies could "take on" any forces that African states either singly or in groups could put on the battlefield. But South Africa's politicians and warlords appear not to realize that the very character of warfare has changed dramatically over the last thirty years and that no country, no matter how militarily powerful, can ever survive a race-war, the sort of war that hangs like a sword of Damocles over South Africa.

The communists are aware, just as every thinking black person at grassroots-level in South Africa is aware, that South Africa contains fatal flaws in her basic makeup as a nation that make her fearsome military might an illusion and dangerous to her.

The type of war being fought today — a terrorist or guerrilla type of war that will make certain forms of heavy present-day military equipment such as tanks and heavy howitzers obsolete within the next twenty years — was made into a fine art by men such as Mao Tse-tung.[158] Such men were adherents of the oriental martial-arts philosophy of using an enemy's might and weight against him, a philosophy that is equally applicable to a single enemy facing you in the centre of the floor of a karate dojo as to an enemy army facing your band of guerrillas on a battlefield.

One of the most devastating tricks used by black terrorist bands in Africa nowadays, a trick they must have learned from Mao Tse-tung and his men, is using the savage killing-power of the target state's armed forces as a weapon to bring about the downfall of that state. And I saw how in Rhodesia's genocidal bush war this trick was used with effect again and again. An army's role is to protect the government and all the people of the country, but an army could easily lose this noble role of protector should it somehow be manipulated into turning its weapons upon the people it is meant to protect.

In Rhodesia a gang of say, three armed terrorists would arrive at a rural kraal or village and either force or persuade the villagers or denizens of the kraal to give them shelter. The terrorists would stay in that place until the security forces got wind of their presence and react with the usual efficiency. Arriving at the village, the soldiers would be met with gunfire and a furious battle would rage; the villagers would panic and start running this way and that, and some of them would run right into the line of fire and get killed.

The surviving villagers and the inhabitants of other villages and kraals nearby, would blame the soldiers, not the terrorists for the deaths and be so enraged as to begin looking upon the soldiers as the enemy and upon the terrorists as friends. A situation that, needless to say, would be exploited by the terrorists to the hilt.

There is growing evidence that the ANC is beginning to manoeuvre the South African Defence Force (SADF) into committing blunders of this kind, especially in the last two cross-border pre-emptive strikes that the SADF launched at ANC targets in Mozambique, Lesotho, Botswana and recently in Zimbabwe. There is something extremely odd in the very recent raids that South Africa launched at three African countries almost at the same time, something that makes me suspect that the ANC led the SADF into a cunningly-laid trap.

The SADF struck at targets in Botswana, Zambia and Zimbabwe and in all those strikes only three people were killed, and for the most part the South Africans appeared to have expended a lot of time, explosives and energy in demolishing uninhabited buildings! If these destroyed buildings had been enemy bases or headquarters one would expect that more people would have been killed. Headquarters of any army conducting a war against a powerful enemy are always heavily-guarded and defended, telephones and radio-sets are manned night and day and there are always high-ranking officers on duty at any given time. But the ANC buildings appeared to have been empty of all this sort of martial activity. Why? I am sure the whole thing was a trap, a very simple trap into which the South Africans blundered head-on.

Now what would be the purpose of such a trap? To bring about the wrath of the West upon South Africa? Perhaps. To force South Africa's hand and make her act in her usual fierce and predictable way at a critical time and so bring about the collapse of delicate negotiations taking place? Perhaps. Well, that too may have been the reason, but I think that there is a much deeper reason, an African reason.

You see, the grassroots-level tribespeople in countries South Africa has repeatedly attacked in the past do not understand the reason behind these attacks and are deeply angered and frightened by them. I have spoken to many Basutho people, ordinary and illiterate peasants and workers, and they one and all cannot understand exactly why South African soldiers have raided their country. Some wrongly assume the South Africans threw their weight behind the rebel forces of Ntsu Mokhehle[159] who had been fighting a low intensity war against the Government of the now deposed Prime Minister Leabua Jonathan[160] for many years. Some believe that the "boers" despise the Basutho and were contemptuous of their King Moshoeshoe II,[161] which is why they occasionally crossed into Lesotho to make war and kill people.

These twisted views of what is to white people of South Africa a straight-forward act of self-defence bode ill for South Africa, for they reveal that the white perception of these raids and the black perception of them are as different as day is to night, and that although the tribal black perception is tainted by ignorance and illiteracy, it is extremely dangerous. When people begin to think that their country and their sovereign are being insulted by what they think is an arrogant, bullying enemy, they tend to do things with great haste and irresponsibility.

I would be the last person to tell South Africa or any other country, not to defend herself against bomb-planting insurgents; but I would warn her to be very careful of how she goes about defending her integrity and sovereignty. At all costs, South Africa must avoid making the mistakes that Rhodesia made.

The Rhodesian Government of Mr Ian Smith blundered horribly throughout the long Rhodesian bush war. The Rhodesian whites, were for the most part, utterly contemptuous of the black man as a thinker, as a fighter and as a human being, and that made them act foolishly and play into the hands of the insurgents again and yet again. Oblivious to the true workings of the black man's mind, his perception of certain things and situations, the Rhodesians fell easy prey to manipulation by black guerrilla leaders, and on well over a hundred occasions that I recorded they were skillfully forced by the terrorists to do their dirty work for them . . . Mao Tse-tung's teachings and African traditional beliefs married together to form a deadly war-weapon.

Let me give you one example out of many. It was the practice of the Rhodesian security forces in the early stages of the bush war to kill black guerrillas and bring their dead bodies into black villages and kraals and exhibit them for a few hours, in a move calculated to fill the villagers with fear of, and respect for, the security forces and which was also intended as a warning to the villagers of just what to expect at the security force's hands should they ever join the terrorists or collaborate with them in any way.

But what the officers of the security forces did not realize was that some of the dead men they exhibited were relatives of some of the villagers, a thing that did not exactly endear the security forces to the people. Also, according to the religious belief of all black tribes in southern Africa if you kill a man fighting for a good cause and then exhibit his body in a public place you actually deify that man in the eyes of his friends, followers or relatives and far from discouraging them from following his example, you actually encourage them to do exactly that.

It was because of mistakes such as this on the part of the Rhodesians and the Smith Government that the insurgent forces of Joshua Nkomo and Robert Mugabe[162] reaped a rich harvest in supporters and followers among the villagers in the bush. And this is why Joshua Nkomo's guerrilla forces for example increased by tens of thousands within a very short time. At the end of that long and bloody war, large areas of Rhodesia were found to be under almost total guerrilla control.

This creation of martyrs to black radicalism and insurgency is the one deadly mistake that South Africa, like Rhodesia before her, has made time and again albeit in different ways. At one time, while I was hiding out in Natal after the destruction of my home in 1976, I tried to warn the late South African Prime Minister, Mr John Vorster,[163] against the danger the rising rate of deaths of detainees in prison posed for South Africa's future. With the assistance of officials of the Natal Midlands Administration Board[164] I made a long recording on two tape cassettes in which I urgently appealed to Mr Vorster and his Government to remove the many soul- crushing grievances that all black people living in South Africa had, grievances directly behind the tragic Soweto Riots of that year.

I minced no words in baring to the Prime Minister the sordid facts of black life in both the urban and rural areas of South Africa, and then I concluded by requesting him to restrain the police in their dealing with prisoners, especially political detainees — because the deaths of such people in detention harmed South Africa and greatly strengthened the hand of black radical extremism in the country.

The tape was sent to Cape Town via the hand of Mr Ritchie Maree of the Midlands Administration Board, and receipt of the tapes was acknowledged in a letter to Mr Maree by Mr Tino Volker, Member of Parliament. The letter, which is in my possession, is dated April 13, 1977.

Mr Vorster must have paid absolutely no attention to my taped pleas because less than six months later Steven Bantu Biko died a horrible death while in detention. The black radicals acquired a new martyr and South Africa's name was besmirched from one end of the civilized world to the other.

Before I came to settle in Bophuthatswana in December 1985 I had the great fortune to meet the South African Deputy Minister of Law and Order, Mr Adrian Vlok, and I appealed to him, this time verbally, just as I had appealed to Mr Vorster by tape so many years ago. I told him about the problems facing blacks in South Africa and that brutality by policemen towards prisoners and political detainees must stop in South Africa's name, because it was turning even the most apolitical and law-abiding black into a sympathizer for black radicalism. Even allegations of these deeds were

125

helping the spread of the communist doctrine amongst black people in South Africa.

I, Credo Vusamazulu Mutwa would gladly die for South Africa, I would die not in order to please the white man and his apartheid system, but I would die to preserve the beauty of this land that mothered me and mine. I would die to preserve the traditional cultures and values of my people regardless of creed, colour or race. But there are things in South Africa that must be stopped, which are wrong in the eyes of God and the eyes of all God-fearing men, things which I cannot in the fullness of my conscience condone or support.

There is far too much corruption and cruelty in South Africa, cruelty perpetrated most often upon the wrong people for the wrong reason, at the wrong time, in the wrong place. I say that this cruelty and this corruption must end if the reform programme the Government has embarked on, is to have any credibility and if the total communistic onslaught upon South Africa and her people is to be halted.

I further say that communism is a carrion-worm that feeds on corruption and fattens on cruelty, and this is one of the reasons why communism is spreading among the black youth in South Africa. But by far the greatest culprits who contribute most to the spread of this abominable philosophy among my people are those people in positions of authority in South Africa, who for years, with brutal deed and irresponsible word, have bred enmity in the hearts of thousands of black men and women for South Africa and the democratic path that she and other Western nations follow.

Thousands of black people believe that under a communistic system of government there is neither exploiter nor exploited, neither high nor low and that all people in communistic controlled countries are treated equally. This is why the name "comrade" has become more and more popular with blacks in the last twenty years. Blacks believe that under communism they all get paid equally regardless of what work they do, that a university professor is paid the same wage as a street-sweeper, and that under this system everybody respects everybody else and no one ever insults or, in any way, degrades a "comrade."

Translated into Zulu, Sotho, Xhosa or any other traditional African language the word "comrade" assumes a far deeper meaning that it has in cold English, and herein lies its danger. Our people hold to an extremely Utopian and highly dangerous view of what communism really is; they have never been told the truth about it, a very unfortunate state of affairs indeed.

Communism is a dead snake with which fools are always scared into toeing a certain line by cunning people throughout the West. Communism is a lie, an illusion and a delusion that over the last sixty years has tried its utmost to look menacing and real and it is by no means the great danger than threatens mankind. One of the many things that I dislike about this nebulous pseudo philosophy is that it readily lends itself to being used by scheming people as a smoke-screen to hide their criminal activities and that it tends to intrude like an unwanted ghost between man and the real dangers that face him, and which threaten his very existence upon the face of the globe.

Communism was not born in hell, nor was it nurtured by the pus-filled udders of Satan's favourite wife in infancy. No, communism was dreamt up by a bearded pauper named Vladimir Lenin[165] who was nurtured with "capitalist" money as he slowly grew from strength to strength. In short, communism is a monster by the very western nations that nowadays claim to be its enemies. And if you do not believe my words then let me ask you just who was it that financed the communist revolutionaries not only before but also during and long after the Russian Revolution? Was it not Max Warburg, a German multimillionaire banker and his American banker brothers.

Communism is nothing more than an ugly mask behind which the rabid bear of Russian imperialism hides its hairy face, to deceive the gullible; and those people who claim to adhere to the empty philosophy of communism are nothing more than pathetic lackeys and lick-spittlings of the Russian nation, which is hell-bent on taking over where the French, British and German empires left off. Just as the West conquered Africa with the assistance of the Bible and the musket, so do the Russians and the Chinese seek to conquer Africa again with the Kalashnikov and the Little Red Book. One has offered Africa a childish myth and the other an empty fraud, so what is the difference?

Communism is a hollow mirage, a god of crumbling rotten aluminium with feet of wet plasticine, which can never exist without corrupt Western "democracies" on which to feed, fatten and grow. This is why all communist-dominated nations are so basically fragile and unstable, and this is why those countries have established an obscene symbiotic existence with the West they revile so much and vociferously claim to hate.

When Hitler invaded Russia during the Second World War Joseph Stalin, that most bloody-handed of modern tyrants, squawked for help and received vast shipments of weapons and food from the very nation that had financed his stinking "Bolshevik"[166] thugs a few decades before — the United States of America. When, recently, the Russians burned their communistic backsides in the Chernobyl[167] nuclear disaster, it did not take them long to come howling for help to mother America and her Allies.

At this very moment, at this very hour, Soviet missile-men are sitting in deep underground shelters, manning missile batteries whose warheads are aimed at western cities. As they sit they are eating bread — bread made of wheat from the vast plains of the USA which sells wheat to these people because their communist system is so inefficient that Russia cannot produce sufficient to feed her enslaved people. I ask myself again and again, why are the Western nations supporting and feeding the monster of communism, which has dedicated itself to devouring them one day . . . ?

Communism can crumble before a barrier of strong spiritual and moral values. It can wilt like an ugly orchid before a firmly united, contented and properly ruled nation whose people are not torn apart by corruption, hunger and disease, as well as petty factional differences.

Like all philosophies that scoff at the spiritual core, such as Muslim fundamentalism possesses, nothing shows the structural weakness of Leninism off more vividly than when the race for the moon was on. It was the Americans who won it by landing living and breathing human beings upon the lunar surface, while the communists managed only an extremely crude and pathetic electronic contraption named Lunakod, to crawl pathetically across the timeless lunar plains before expiring like a foul abortion.

As for South Africa being a bastion against communism, well, let me ask but one question. Why then has she, over the last thirty years, made a series of terrible mistakes that brought the rapid spreading of the communist philosophy among her black population?

24

Showing Our Children the Way

Firstly, let me reveal to you that terrorism is nothing new to Africa, because there were terrorist groups in Natal in the last century that employed many of the methods of intimidating and terrorizing people that modern terrorist groups and organizations employ in South Africa.

If you look at a map of Natal you will find a small town named Congella, a town that stands on the site of one of the Zulu king, Shaka's, military kraals, known as Kwa-Khangela, a Zulu word which means "observe" and which the British people corrupted to Congella.

The full name of this great fortress-kraal was Kwa Khangela-Amankengane, which means "the place of observing the deviating people" and its history is very interesting indeed. Just as the white man over the centuries has developed a number of creeds and philosophies by which tens of thousands of people still live and die even today, so has the black man of Africa developed large numbers of philosophies in the course of the years. Many of these philosophies have died out in the course of time; but many are still kept alive by followers throughout Africa.

Few philosophies in Africa could ever match, for sheer strangeness, that of the people whom the Zulus of Natal were soon to know as the *Amankengane,* a name which means "they who deviate from the path." White writers of South African history give a completely wrong translation of the name "Amankengane," they translate it as "vagabonds" but it has nothing to do with vagabonds whatsoever.

When the great King Dingiswayo's long reign was drawing to a close, there suddenly arose from the Tonga people of the north of Zululand a wild-eyed mystic named Mgombane who began preaching a strange new doctrine. Mgombane taught people that man was born a free creature and that people who saddled him with laws, rules and customs were wrong.

He taught that no man had the right to call himself king or chief over others, no man had the right to own anything and that people ought to be allowed to do whatsoever they wish with their lives, because, after all, a human being was born alone and should live whatever life he or she wanted without being dictated to by anybody. Mgombane also taught that if a person wished to pursue the life of a drunkard or dagga-addict he or she could go ahead and do so, and that the wearing of ornaments was silly and the cleansing of one's body in water often was absurd.

Mgombane's preachings caught on like a bush fire among the malcontents and the youth of many tribes in Natal. Soon he was followed and hailed as a saviour by hundreds of noisy, unwashed and drunken men, women and even children, every one of them a fugitive from the highly regimented and disciplined life of that time. People were compelled to bathe at least once on winter days and thrice on hot days, and the smoking of dagga and the drinking of beer by people under the age of twenty years were strictly taboo.

Soon Mgombane's followers acquired a name among the tribes throughout Natal, they became known either as the Iziyendane, that is "the drunken staggerers" or the Amankengane; that is "they who deviate from the path."

So rapidly did Mgombane's philosophy spread and so vast became the number of people who flocked to join it, that King Dingiswayo decided to take action and crush this new creed that was threatening the stability of his empire. Dingiswayo first tried to use force against the Amankengane and he failed because these wild people had absolutely no respect for the honored rules of warfare. They fought dirty, luring Dingiswayo's regiments into dense bush, where the warriors were forced to abandon their tight battle formation and split into small groups which the Amankengane happily destroyed piecemeal by the simple method of stabbing each warrior from

130

behind. It was only by adopting some of their own dirty fighting tactics that this great king's warriors were able to vanquish these anarchists in three great battles.

Dingiswayo realized, after his third and greatest victory over Mgombane's followers, that it was the harsh life that his people led that caused them to escape and join the Deviating People, and he set about making the life of his subjects as exciting and as beautiful as possible. He created great sporting events in which everybody was free to take part, be it a man, a woman or a child. He encouraged arts such as pottery making, wood and ivory carving, bead making and metal-work on a massive scale giving prizes of cattle, sheep and goats to the best craftspeople in the land. To this day the most beautiful artifacts in wood, ivory and metal ever produced by the Zulu speaking people of Natal were created during the reign of this great and enlightened king.

Dingiswayo realized that the only way he could save his people from the snare of Mgombane's philosophy was by building up his people's spiritual resistance to this madman's preachings as well as give prominence to the positive and creative side of the tribal way of life.

It is said that some months after the last great battle in which he crushed the Amankengane for the third time, Dingiswayo captured the anarchist leader himself, and after Dingiswayo had passed the death sentence upon him Mgombane demanded the right to execute himself, saying that his life was his own and no one had the right to end it, save himself. Thereupon Mgombane climbed a tree with a rope of plaited goat-skin, tied one end of the rope to a stout branch and calmly fitted the noose around his neck and jumped.

After Dingiswayo's death it was King Shaka who inherited the Amankengane problem, because no sooner had the great King Dingiswayo died than the Deviating People got up to their tricks again. They cut a swathe of devastation through Shaka's territory, cutting off people's upper lips, ears and even abducting women and impaling men and children on kraal palisades.

Many of the methods of terrorizing people employed by modern black terrorists nowadays, methods such as mutilating a man's cattle, cutting off people's upper lips, ears and even genitals with pangas were first employed by people such as the hated drunken people known as the Amankengane.

King Shaka acted with characteristic swiftness and fury, learning that the Amankengane were now hiding in dense bush near the Umfolozi River. He sent three crack regiments against them, tricked them into attacking one of the regiments in the open, away from the sheltering bush and caught them in a deadly trap using the two other regiments . . . and massacred them.

Afterwards Shaka ensured against the resurgence of the Amankengane menace by building strongholds in strategic places throughout Zululand and filled them with some of his best warriors and trackers in order to deal with the small groups of Deviating People that had escaped the massacre and were now skulking in remote areas in the land of the Zulus.

As the years passed the Amankengane bands became smaller and smaller as hunger and disease took their toll on the Unwashed Ones and finally they vanished from the doorstep of Zulu history forever.

There is a lesson for all of us today in the way King Dingiswayo and King Shaka dealt with the Amankengane philosophy and so saved the nation from succumbing to Mgombane's insanity. This is how I feel we ought to deal with the creeping menace of communism in South Africa . . . by showing our children the positive side of the western democratic way of life as quickly as we can and by so strengthening the minds of all our people, this Godless menace will never be able to penetrate the shining armour of truth with which they would then be arrayed. There are things in this world against which force of arms alone are useless, things that can only be defeated by weapons of the soul.

25

My People, Come Back

What is happening to the black people of South Africa today is by no means unusual, rather it is something that happened hundreds of times to conquered people since the very dawn of human history.

When a defeated people reach the stage of spiritual, mental and physical disintegration that the black people of South Africa have reached; when many signs start appearing that reveal that these people are heading for national or racial suicide; when the people start showing an unnatural aggressiveness, suspicion and fear; when thousands of them start falling apart as a result of overindulgence in liquor and drugs; and when sacred institutions such as marriage start falling to pieces; then it is the time for enlightened men and women to appear from among those people who will take the whole race, the whole nation, by the shoulder and show it a new direction. A new direction leading towards self-discovery and self-respect, and because no one is doing this for the black people of this country then I, Credo Mutwa, intend to try and do so.

The South African black man is heading for racial suicide; he is being betrayed by his leaders who are feeding him bitterness and rage when they should be feeding him hope and self-understanding; he is being betrayed by self-seekers who are pushing petrol bombs and rocks into his hands and urging him to go out and perish. My people are being betrayed by foreign dogs who are thrusting Russian guns and bombs into their hands and bidding them to go forth and die, die not for the memory of Shaka or Dingiswayo, but for the blood-drenched name of one pederast named Vladimir Ilyich Lenin.

The black man of South Africa does not know his true greatness, he does not know there are things the white man has only recently discovered that his forefathers knew about hundreds of years ago. He does not know that within him lies coiled a beautiful serpent, a golden dragon which could, if released, soar to the stars tomorrow and make the black people of our country as respected and as powerful as the Japanese.

I call to you, all my people throughout South Africa; I call to you in the sunset days of my life; come back, away from death and destruction, come back and let me show you a new way, a way to salvation for all of us, and a way you can gain all you desire without shedding a single drop of human blood, be it your children's, yours or anyone else's.

I know that many of you have absolutely no wish to see our country drown in blood, you have no desire whatsoever to see all that you hold obliterated by the howling storms of war and the shrieking tempests of battle. You seek only to be treated like human beings in a human world, you seek only that the white man stops despising you and heaping oppressive laws upon your heads, laws that apply only to you and not to people of other races. You want to take part in the decision-making process of your country, and you do not want to be deceived and fobbed off with Machiavellian tricks such as Separate Development has clearly turned out to have been.

My people, you can gain all these things and much, much more if you only listen to what I have to say, but before I reveal my suggestions to you, I beg you to listen to this little story, the true story of a people that achieved more by peaceful means than it has achieved by bloody war.

For many decades after its discovery by the West, the Far Eastern nation known as Japan deliberately surrounded itself with a thick mist of isolation, seeking to protect its people and their religion and culture against the destructive and destabilizing influences from the West. For many decades Western nations held the Japanese in cold contempt and this became extremely hurtful to these ancient people, and it was as a direct result of this attitude on the part of some Western nations, that Japan soon began adopting Western civilization and Western technology on a large scale. Japan became warlike, seeking to assert her rights and her existence as a nation and she went to war with Russia, a gnat taking on a mighty elephant; and in 1905 the Japanese Navy inflicted a severe and humiliating defeat upon the Imperial Russian Navy in the Tsushima Straits.

But still the West did not give Japan the respect that was her due, they said the Japanese were a nation of copyists who were totally incapable of inventing anything on their own, and there came a time when anything that was marked as having been made in Japan was treated as a joke by the West. Japan went to war with China and brought that vast country to its knees, and then she made the mistake of going to war not only with the British Empire but also with the mightly United States of America. She was horribly, shatteringly defeated and furthermore she received the first two nuclear blows ever dealt a country in human history and was beaten to her knees.

But Japan today rules the world with her cars, ships and transistor-radios; her Nissan, Honda and Toyota vehicles have routed American Fords, Cadillacs, De Sotos and Chevrolets from the streets and highways of the Western world. Her watches gleam around millions of wrists from London to Addis Ababa and from Baghdad to Los Angeles.

Japan, the envy of her former enemies and a future world power second to none . . . and the black people of South Africa can easily follow her shining example. And why do I say this seemingly incredible thing? Japan's secret is that she married the old and the new with consummate skill. She drew equally from the rich golden well of her ancient culture as from the electronic pool of western technology. Japan used that mixture as fuel to propel herself from the position of a defeated and weakened nation to that of a smiling and triumphant industrial giant.

And as the Japanese did, so can you, my people; because although many of you are unaware of this, your forefathers left you a vast treasure-trove of knowledge that could lead you to the very stars tomorrow, knowledge that could place you in the forefront of the world's most respected nations and make your sufferings of the present times things of the long-forgotten past.

Today, in great laboratories in the USA and the USSR, scientists are spending millions of dollars and roubles on top-secret experiments with what white people term the "paranormal," namely things such as telepathy, telekinesis and extra sensory perception (ESP). In Czechoslovakia a man named Robert Pavlita[168] is building and experimenting with what he calls "psychotronic devices," which are mysterious metal devices that obtain their power from the mysterious powers of the human mind; but these devices, we are told, are intended for use in future wars.

But wait: telepathy, telekinesis and ESP are things that are well known to the black people, things that thousands of sangomas and inyangas have used for hundreds of years. When a sangoma uses her powers to locate a child lost for several hours in the African bush and to even tell the child's parents which route to take in order to reach their child quickest, the power she has used to see where that child is, is ESP, a phenomenon the white man is still struggling to learn to use.

When a sanusi sends an unspoken message to another sanusi across a great distance, begging him or her to come quickly, the power he uses is called telepathy in English; and when a sangoma uses her "spiritual hand" to remove an object stuck in the throat of a child without touching the child, the power used is telekinesis. So the black man is far ahead of the white man in this knowledge, and if an imaginative and far-sighted African head-of-state were to collect a group of sangomas and sanusis and send them to the USA to assist those American scientists who are doing research into the paranormal, those sangomas and sanusis would make a dramatic contribution to this new and extremely important field of science that would enable the USA to surge far ahead in parapsychological research.

Many years ago I was visited in my Diepkloof home by the famous young Israeli named Uri Geller who proceeded to give me and my sangoma followers a demonstration of his powers. When the impressive display was over the sangomas laughed, and so did I. I then told this talented young Israeli that people with powers identical to his, were still quite common among us black people of South Africa, because a large majority of us still live close to nature and have lost none of the great gifts that God gave to our forebears in the remotest antiquity, gifts that enabled human beings to survive in a prehistoric world that was a thousand times more hostile towards humanity than it is now.

I went on to tell Mr Geller that it was my opinion that things such as telepathy were originally part of man's survival aparatus in remote times, and that one group of hunter-gatherer human beings could use telepathy to warn other groups in the vicinity about a coming danger such as the sudden and violent flooding of a great river.

Also, a lone human being in the winderness, dying in agony after having eaten the berries of a tree he or she had stumbled across could use telepathy to send a warning to relatives far away to avoid the berries.

I then ordered our most junior sangoma, Maggie Ndhlovu of Diepkloof Zone Five in Soweto, to give Mr Geller and the newspaper reporters a small demonstration of traditional African mind power. We locked this short, fat and dark-skinned girl in my bedroom with pen and paper and left the house after drawing the curtains so that Maggie was completely alone inside.

In the garden I asked Mr Geller to draw a number of designs on a piece of paper and then when he had done this I too took the paper and drew three designs on it — and then we waited. About half an hour went by before we heard a tapping on one window-pane, this being the agreed signal to us from Maggie that she had completed her task.

She opened the window as I walked towards the house and I, without looking at the paper, took it over to Mr Geller and the reporters. Mr Geller's beautiful dark eyes narrowed with amazement and he handed the paper over to a reporter who gasped with astonishment as he compared the paper on which Mr Geller and I had drawn figures to the one Maggie had handed me. The young sangoma had reproduced *all* our figures with uncanny accuracy — a Star of David and a solar system symbol drawn by Mr Geller, a German car trademark, a hut and a linx's head drawn by me.

This episode in my life, together with many others like it, prove beyond all doubt that Africa has something of great importance to give to the world, something that if properly organized, could bring in millions of dollars to the starving people of South Africa. But there is more, much much more that can help the black man to gain dignity and freedom and respect in the eyes of other nations and ultimately lead him and the rest of humanity to the stars and beyond.

There are many great secrets that actually survive in Africa and are known to sanusis and juju-priests and priestesses, and one of these secrets is that of hammering and tempering copper in secret hot fluids and so make it even harder than steel, a secret that was known to the ancient Egyptians who used copper chisels tempered in this way to shape the great blocks of stone with which their temples and pyramids were built.

This secret, which would be worth millions of dollars today, is known in central Africa by traditional blacksmiths who use it to make small sacrificial knives used in sacred rituals. I learned the secret from a Baganda blacksmith[169] near the Murchison Falls in Uganda. I first had to swear a solemn oath before a group of Baganda and Kavirondo blacksmiths[170] and traditional healers before I could be entrusted with the ancient secret of tempering copper, an oath in which I swore never to pass on the secret to other men, only to other African sanusis like myself.

Some three years later, this time in the then Tanganyika Territory, I took yet another oath, an oath a hundred times more terrible than the first, this time before an old Wagogo[171] traditional blacksmith and his sons. I was about to be entrusted with two strange secrets, the secret of making blue glass that does not break and also the secret of making and tempering a fantastic kind of steel known to blacksmiths as muwudzi, a steel that I feel could change the course of African history and bring great wealth to this impoverished continent.

A knife made from muwudzi is a fantastic sight; it looks as if it is made out of silver, so bright is the metal; and it looks, at the same time, as if it is made of frozen watered silk. It is so sharp that you can use it to split a flamingo's feather from top to bottom. A muwudzi blade can only be tempered in the body of a living animal, which is why it is heated almost red-hot and then driven into the heart of a sacrificial bull during the sacred "Manyandisa-Shatti"[172] ceremony before being thrown into a river or a lake and lost forever. Once used this way the blade must never again be used for any other profane purpose, and so such holy knives are made only for the slaying of the sacred bull during this secret ceremony.

The blacksmith who taught me these secrets told me that the first people to make weapons of muwudzi steel were the Arab slave traders who used black labour to smelt this mystical metal in large quantities, to make swords for the warriors of Salah-al-Din.[173] The blacksmith told me that some of the slaves employed in the making of this magical metal escaped, taking the secrets of the steel into the interior of Tanganyika with them.

My people: I am positive that even in these days of space-age metals, glass of all kinds and many other scientific marvels there must be a place for African traditional discoveries in the great markets of the world. I am sure that once the world has discovered, or found a use for these things from our remote past and even now, it would beat a well-worn path to Africa's door and our country; and the people would be as respected as the people of the Land of the Rising Sun are today.

I appeal to all of you alive in South Africa, before we plunge into the fiery lake of war, please let us first give *peace* a chance. I do not say these words out of cowardice, for those who know me know I am no coward. I am not saying these words because I happen to be a traitor because those closest to me know that I am no traitor, but I am saying them because I do not wish to see my country die. I do not wish to see my people perish because once my country has died and my people have perished what then shall I be? Once a great tree has been reduced to ashes in a great forest fire what becomes of the few surviving leaves that drift in the weeping wind?

I know that my people are frustrated, bitter and angry, but I also know that taking them by the scruff of the neck and pushing them into the thrice-fired furnace of war is not the right thing to do. SUCH A PEOPLE NEED TO BE STRENGTHENED SPIRITUALLY AND REBUILT, AND NOT OBLITERATED.

26

Mankind . . . One Big Family?

One of the many things that has added to my anguish was a discovery I had made in the course of my journeys to the reservations of these beautiful mysterious people known to the world as Red Indians. It was a discovery so strange I could not bring myself to believe the evidence of my eyes and ears.

I had found that some Red Indian tribes such as the Hopi, the Paiute, the Navajo, the Cherookee and even the proud Sioux — in fact all Indian tribes in the USA and Indians of other countries, such as Mexico — had astonishing linguistic and cultural links with black tribes in Africa! I had collected a list of the customs that these tribes had in olden times and which they still practice in remote parts of the American continent. I found that these customs corresponded exactly with those of many tribes in Africa whose territories I had visited during my long travels.

For example: I found that a Red Indian medicine-man goes through an illness similar to the illness a Zulu sangoma goes through before being initiated. Like a sangoma a Red Indian "shaman" has "out-of-body" experiences, sees similar visions and hears similar voices directing his actions. Like an African "medicine-man" the Red Indian medicine-man burns a special greyish-green herb called "sage" to drive away evil influences. The greyish-green herb that Zulu inyangas burn is called "Mpepho" and although it is different from sage it nevertheless has a similar smell when burnt.

Many Red Indian fables are uncannily similar to African fables with only very slight differences here and there. For example, in some Red Indian fables the coyote is the hero, and the jackal is the hero in the African version. In fables where the bear plays a major part among the Red Indians the gorilla takes that part in the African version.

Among some warlike Red Indian tribes there was a custom called "counting a coup" in which you merely touched an enemy warrior with your weapon without killing him. Swazis have a similar custom, and so do the Zulus, especially in friendly stick-fighting where a touch with the stick is counted as a blow.

The Zulus also had a war-custom in which a badly wounded warrior, or a warrior who had sworn never to return alive from a battle, deliberately tied his ankles with lengths of cowhide to thick stakes driven into the ground so that he would die where he stood, without moving an inch. Warlike Red Indian tribes such as the Cheyennes, or the Shyelas as they really call themselves, had a very similar custom called "staking one's self out" in which a brave staked himself to the ground.

Red Indians paid a bride price of horses to the bride-to-be's father exactly as Zulus and other African tribes pay the "lobola" in cattle to the father of one's wife-to-be. There were usually nine horses for the Red Indian girl, just as there are nine head of cattle for the Zulu girl.

In the language of the Navajo, a stone is called *"tse"* and in Zulu it is called *"tshe"* or *"itshen."* In the language of the Cherookes a father is called *"udoda"* and in Zulu a married man is called *"ndoda"* or *"indoda."* In the now fast dying out language of the Paiutes, a lizard is called a *"nobu"* and in the language of the Tswana people of Botswana and in the Transvaal a chameleon is known as a *"leobu"* — and in Zulu it is called a *"nwabu."*

During my stay in the United States I collected well over two thousand Red Indian words that resembled African words. But there are other, more amazing resemblances: this time in Central America.

The Mayan[174] of ancient times, believed in a great legendary hero named Kukulkan who came in a reed boat from the East and found the Mayan living like beasts in holes in the ground. Kukulkan taught them respect and things like how to build proper homes, how to worship the gods and how to have laws. The Zulu people of South Africa believe in a similar hero named Khulu-Khukwana who name is often confused with that of God, Nkulunkulu, by ignorant anthropologists. Khulu-Khukwana, according to Zulu legend, also arrived from across the sea from the East, in a great reed raft and found the Zulus living like lawless beasts in caves and on tree-tops. And he also taught them how to make fire, how to build huts, to have laws and how to keep livestock.

Exactly like the Mayan's Kukulkan, the Zulu hero Khulu-khukwana was driven to alcoholism by trying to keep peace among warring human factions for many years, and he became so frustrated in the end that he got onto his raft and sailed away, promising to return only on the day "zebras started growing horns on their heads like goats."

The miracle does not end here, because when I went to Japan in 1985 I found astonishing linguistic and cultural similarities between the black people of Africa and the Japanese people.

For example in Japanese, fire is called *hie* and in Tsonga heat is called *hisa* and in Zulu *shisa*. In Japanese a long, slightly-curving one-edged sword is called a *katana* and in Zaire a similar weapon or a machete is called a *katanga*. In Japanese a stone is called *ishi*, and in Zulu, *itshe*. I could go on and on for page after page . . . .

But let me say this, the discoveries I made in the USA and Japan regarding the strange similarities that exist between the culture and languages of the people of those countries and Africa added to the discovery that similarities exist between ancient and even modern European — as well as Hindu and even Polynesian and Melanesian languages and cultures — and these of Africa. And this proves to me conclusively that mankind is not only one great family, but also at one time in the past shared a common language, a common religion and a common culture and that the division of human beings into different races — a thing that caused the advent of racism and all that goes with it — is really a fairly recent phenomenon, a dangerous accident of evolution.

I say there are stories told by old men and women around tribal cooking-fires throughout the world that are the same no matter where you go. Some of these stories have over the centuries become enshrined in secret scrolls and even in books such as the Bible. I say that it is time we looked at these stories with new eyes because fantastic and far-fetched though they may seem at first sight, childish though they may seem to cold-hearted skeptics with atrophied minds, *these tales could be true — and are true.*

The Bible, for example, says there was a time when men spoke one language and when they built a great tower called the Tower of Babel; and tried to use it to climb to Heaven. So great a threat did God view this to be He destroyed the tower and scattered human beings all over the face of the earth.

I say that this story is true — at least in part. Evidence that at one time people were united by culture and language is too solid, too overwhelming to be ignored even by the most brutish of doubting Thomases. The Bible also states something that has been supported by overwhelming archeological evidence, that God created people near three great rivers, the Euphrates, the Tigris and one other river known as "the river Gihon, which flowed through Ethiopia."

I have not been able to pinpoint the river Gihon, but I do know that in parts of that country, as well as in parts of Kenya known as Olduvai Gorge, scientists have found the remains of different kinds of human beings, the oldest dating back to well over three million years ago and the youngest dating to only a few thousand years. Did a great river once flow through this region, a river that left its traces as far south as Tanganyika and Kenya in the form of great gorges? Perhaps.

Here is another interesting thing that we find in the Bible, the incredible statement that "the serpent was the most intelligent creature in those times." A serpent cleverer than man, clever enough to get the first two human beings on earth in trouble with the Creator? Logical if you consider that there is undisputable archeological evidence that reptiles were created before man on this planet. The biblical story is supported by African mythology in which again and again you find story-tellers attributing to snakes an intelligence far greater than that of us humans.

Venda mythology furthermore tells us that it was a python that taught the first man and woman how to make love; and so does Baluba, Chokwe, Kavirondo and even Khoisan mythology.

Why would ancient people believe in something so odd as that snakes were wiser than us at one time? Because the lizard and the serpent crawled upon the face of the world long before we were ever heard of.

Among the many strange stories we find all over the world, is the tale of a great flood and a wise old man who built either a raft or an ark. With this ark he, his friends and family, as well as different species of animals, birds and insects were able to survive while the rest of the world drowned. This story I have found all over Africa and in other parts of the world.

There are also stories of a whole continent that was destroyed both by fire and by water and which sank forever under the sea. The Red Indians called it Aztlan, the Greeks called it Atlantis and African people call it Amariri or Amurire — the Land of the Dying Sun.

There are even stories that appear to plumb the depths of fantasy and madness, and which are the last kind of story one would logically expect to find among earthbound primitive people who had neither telescopes nor flying machines, stories of destroyed planets and not just continents, stories of creatures that came out of the skies in flying contraptions of all kinds, from flying calabashes of monstrous size, made out of silver to flying grain-baskets woven not of grass but of copper-wire or gold-wire.

There are stories I have found throughout Africa that tell that man was not created upon this world but on another world that orbits a star untold distances away. In one version the story is told of a weird creature named Ngcezu by the Zulus. It goes like this:

There was a great famine in the land. Rain had not fallen for many moons and the people were starving. The men were weak and no longer able to move and the women and children reduced to wrinkled skeletons that moved weakly among the huts of the villages, searching for food where no food was to be found. The chief of the tribe, in order to try and save his surviving people, was forced to slaughter the sacred beasts, a white cow and a black bull — sacred to the ancestral spirits — and shared their flesh among his people.

"The ancestral spirits will not be angry with us," said the chief to his people, "for we are nearly dead with hunger and so the sacred beasts must die so that we may live. But please preserve the ears of both the cow and the bull and hang them to dry in the Ancestral Shrine."

Then one night the great chief saw a great fire in the skies and a great star fell to the ground and set the bush on fire. The Chief was not afraid so he took his shield and assegai and went to investigate. As he drew close to the fire he saw a creature emerge from the flames and come walking towards him. A strange creature that was like a man but with burning yellow eyes, a great gash of a mouth and a great red comb like that of a cock on its big sky-blue head. The creature greeted the chief with a raised hand and a fearsome crocodile-like smile and it told the chief it was coming in peace and its name was Ngcezu the Star Magician.

"What ails your people, O Chief?" asked Ngcezu. "Why are they dying in such large numbers?"

"My people are hungry O Ngcezu," replied the Chief. "The rain has not fallen for a long time and the cattle have died and there is no food left in the land."

"Then I shall help you, great Chief," said Ngcezu, "I shall make the rain fall, and the trees and the grass as well as the grain shall grow!"

Ngcezu gestured with his hands towards the skies and immediately the clouds gathered. The thunder roared and the rain began to fall in torrents. Then, in the chief's village Ngcezu caused a great shining pot to appear out of nowhere and he asked the women of the village to fill the great pot with water and to leave it in the centre of the village. Ngcezu stopped the rain and the sun shone for a few moments. When the sun shone upon the magic pot the water changed into delicious food that the people had never seen before.

The Star Magician told the people to dish the food out of the pot and to eat and then carry some of the food to all the villages in the land. And so for days Ngcezu fed the tribe while the grain grew and the grass and the trees became green once more.

Then one day Ngcezu asked the chief to bring out the ears of the two beasts and to put them in the great magic pot, and after they had done that the pot grew larger and larger and then out of its mouth there emerged hundreds of young cows and young bulls identical to the beasts that had been eaten; and the herds of the tribe began to spread through the land. The villages had milk and meat once more.

The grain ripened and the people had a great harvest that they celebrated with much feasting, singing and dancing. While the people feasted the chief turned to Ngcezu who was the guest of honour and asked him just how the tribe could reward him for all the good he had done. Ngcezu replied that as a reward he would only like to claim a small thing, and when he had said this the chief and all his elders roared their agreement that Ngcezu could claim anything, anything whatsoever, he wished.

But some days after this the tribes-people came to the chief to complain most bitterly, they complained that although Ngcezu had stated that he had only wanted a "small thing" he had actually tricked the tribe by not telling them exactly what he wanted as a reward. He was storming like a bull from village to village and noisily raping any woman he managed to catch.

"Our womenfolk have sought refuge in dense bush and even on the summits of high mountains, O Chief," complained the tribespeople, "but even there they are not safe from Ngcezu. He hunts them down, chases and rapes them, laughing like a delighted hyena!"

While the people were speaking there came sounds of a fearful commotion in the direction of the chief's village — from the women's quarters. Loud screams of terror and insane laughter rang through the village and the chief and the people hurried to investigate. There they found the chief's favourite wife struggling in the lecherous arms of the Star Magician, who was ravishing her with unearthly delight while the other members of the chief's harem scattered in all directions like helpless sheep.

Battle-axe in hand the chief roared with jealous rage, seized Ngcezu by the penis and lopped of that mischievous organ with one swing of the axe.

"Oh you evil, ungrateful human being!," cried Ngcezu in great agony, "I should have known better than to come and help creatures like you! You have deprived me of the only thing that really means anything to me and now it is going to take me a thousand years to grow a new one in its place. I am leaving you now and neither you nor your tribe will ever see me again!" And so saying Ngcezu vanished before their eyes!

To this day when a lazy Zulu girl leaves a cooking-pot unattended in the fireplace, her mother or her sister always angrily asks her the following question: "Why have you left this pot unattended? Do you think it is Ngcezu's pot that it can attend to itself?"

Also, when a good person who has done much for other people gets rewarded with evil by them, the Zulus will always say: "Yebo, ngisho no Ngcezu bamqamula umthondo — Yes, even Ngcezu had his penis slashed off."

This is but one of hundreds of such stories that we find among the Zulu people and other Nguni-speaking tribes in Natal and the Cape. These stories do not stand alone, but stand side by side with knowledge black people could only have acquired from extraterrestrial sources, knowledge hundreds of years ahead of any knowledge that even the West possesses at present.

My people the Zulus and the Sotho-speaking and Tsonga-speaking tribes of South Africa possess knowledge about germs and bacteria that is astonishing and they had a name in their particular language long before the white man came to South Africa, a name that often described the shape of the organisms. In Zulu germs are known as the *"amagciwane"* a name which means "the tiniest living creatures." In Tsonga germs are known as *"ntsonga-ntsongana* — an amazing word that means "spiral-spiral creatures," which is the shape of germs that cause venereal disease.

Sotho speakers call germs by another amazing name which is *"dinonokana,"* a name which means "tiny, treacherous tormentors." Black people throughout southern Africa made crude antibiotics, which they used in treating infection. They made these antibiotics by mashing fresh maize-break into claypots and then placing the pots in a dark place until a furry mould formed over the mess, and this cobweb-like mould was the antibiotic.

All tribes throughout the parts of Africa that I have visited possess an uncanny knowledge of stars, worlds and planets other than our own; and even the bushmen in the Kalahari and in Namibia know — please do not ask me how — that the moon has plains, valleys and mountains. Furthermore, bushmen told me their eyes were sharp enough to *see* the great mountains on the surface of the moon and to see that there were no rivers or life up there.

What I have done in this chapter is attempt to show you very briefly some of the mysteries behind Africa and all her people. I am only showing you the barest bones of some of the tremendous knowledge that would be forever lost if southern Africa is allowed to drown in a race war. The amazing knowledge, most of it never before recorded, that would be lost to mankind if the Red Indians are allowed to fade into the mists of oblivion.

I am showing you very briefly some of the knowledge being lost to future generations because of rampant racism in all countries on earth nowadays. Make no mistake about this, racism is the greatest danger that threatens peace on earth, racism is the only thing and the only one that can cause nations to employ nuclear weapons against each other without any restraint whatsoever. Racism turns even the most moderate and God-fearing person into a raging beast, it exploits the basest, most bestial fears in the human reptilian mind. And although it may have had some evolutionary use in remote pre-history, it is now a foul and dangerous atavism that should be eradicated, an atavism that has long outlived its purpose.

I say mankind stands poised on the brink of the most monumental scientific discoveries of its history, discoveries that could alter our view of creation and the universe and mankind's origin radically for all time. I say that human beings of all races must urgently join hands and make the world safe for future generations and for the peaceful pursuit of science — one of God's greatest gift to humankind.

Some weeks ago I was visited in my new Bophuthatswana home by an American scientist and industrialist, Dr Jim Hurtak,[175] President of the Future Sciences Organization. The doctor showed me unretouched photographs sent back to earth from the planet Mars by an American space-probe.

The photographs showed gorges, craters and volcanoes upon the face of the red planet and they also showed huge structures that could only have been made by intelligent creatures. Gigantic pyramid-like structures that cast faultlessly triangular shadows upon the battered surface of Mars. But there was more: a gigantic face the Americans described as "a monkey's face" looking up at the heavens from the alien plains, a face that I immediately recognized as Negroid judging from the shadow that it casts upon the ground.

Against such awesome discoveries does not our petty quarrelsomeness fall away. Does not our religious and racial chauvinism seem not only stupid and squalid but also frankly criminal. I say that great discoveries wait to be made in the next twenty years or so and I also say that side by side with these great discoveries there will come deadly dangers as well.

New diseases caused by new chemical substances, or even by mutant strains of bacteria, will stalk the earth, or old diseases will suddenly reappear in new and virulent forms, such as AIDS, which was confined to central Africa for years; but which has now suddenly changed into a fast spreading, vicious killer for hitherto unknown reasons.

In order to meet these and other great challenges of the future, people need to banish racism and many other negative and childish "isms" and join hands like true children of one parent.

27

Ghettos, Townships, Development and Homelands

I have tried to reveal many things to you about South Africa — things that are known to only a few people who live in this troubled country of ours. I have no magic solution to offer my country and I do not intend to join the ranks of those who have dished out political solutions to South Africa's problems left, right and centre.

Over the years South Africa's name has become so thickly overlaid with a patina of misinformation and propaganda, both for and against her, that it is essential for anyone seeking the hidden truth behind what is happening in this unhappy country at present, to first work hard at scraping off the crust like a patient archeologist before the untarnished facts can shine through. Before I close this book there are a few important subjects I feel need to be made clear to all — and I shall proceed to do just that as briefly and as clearly as I am able to.

Here we go.

There are many people both in South Africa and abroad that say that South Africa is filled with ghettoes and that the various black homelands are just dumping grounds for thousands of blacks endorsed out of the cities and where malnutrition and all manner of diseases thrive.

No, South Africa is not filled with ghettoes. There are vast township complexes like Soweto, KwaMashu, Thembisa and Khaya-litsha, and vast squatter camps such as Crossroads; and if these places were properly developed by imaginative and courageous people, they would quickly grow into real cities with industries, highways and even railways.

Although it *is* true that the townships are haunted by all manner of official inefficiency and corruption, and although it is true that human lives are a cent-a-dozen in these places, they are paradises of cleanliness and order compared to the "Favelas"[176] of Rio De Janeiro and other South American cities. In these places one's astonished eyes are greeted by literally hundreds of tumbled-down and vermin-haunted hovels of all sizes. Some are built of wood floating above the ground on stilts and others are built of corrugated iron, canvas or cardboard . . . all jumbled up shoulder to shoulder like drunken soldiers along narrow, winding and rutted streets — ankle-deep in filth. Inhabiting these hovels are thousands of white, black, Indian and half-caste people of all ages. People without hope, people without employment and people mostly without a future.

South Africa's vast black townships at least have, with only a few exceptions here and there, water-borne sewerage, clean tapwater, organized refuse-removal, clinics, schools, supermarkets and sports fields. Many of these townships have tall mast-lights to light up their streets and many houses have electricity. In revealing all this I am not playing an Uncle Tom, patting the South African Government on the back, I am only stating facts as I know them.

I am a well travelled man who has seen several countries in the last ten years or so and I can make clear comparisons on many things. Only once during my travels did I see a place that more than deserved the name of "black ghetto." A place uglier and far dirtier than Alexandra Township in Johannesburg, a stinking, sodden place of abysmal misery where hundreds of people live in multi-storey buildings, condemned as unfit for human habitation many grey decades ago. Buildings with neither doors nor windows, nothing but gaping squares and oblongs of cold emptiness through which the icy wind and the weeping sleet pours in with unrelenting fury . . . .

To the dark ending of my earthly days, I shall remember the hideous place known as Harlem in New York City. I shall remember the stench, the crime, the degradation and the brutality; but I shall also, thankfully, remember the kindness and the courage and gaiety of some of the many lost souls that inhabit that icy hell on earth.

Regarding the black homelands, no one can deny that there is hunger and disease and misery in many of these places, that there are hundreds of people here who can only afford to eat a small bowlful of maize-meal porridge a day, who count themselves lucky to see a piece of meat once in two months and who have become stunted both bodily and intellectually by years of undernourishment.

No one can deny, for example, that there are parts of Zululand, such as Umsinga, where starving Zulus shoot you dead in cold blood if they see you bringing food of any kind from the cities to your wife and children. Your children have no right to eat all that food while their children go hungry, they say. I know two men who were killed within a few days of each other for no reason other than that they had a habit of bringing large bags of maize meal and other foodstuffs home to Umsinga when on leave.

However, the plight of the thousands of suffering black people in the homelands has not gone unnoticed by either the South African Government or the South African public in general, because for years now we have had organizations such as Kupugani,[177] Operation Snowball[178] and Operation Hunger,[179] to name but three, that have done much towards alleviating the suffering of our people in the homelands and the urban areas.

The Kupugani organization for instance sent tons of soup powder, dried milk and dehydrated vegetables, beans, sugar and mealie-meal to each one of our homelands for distribution among the poor and the hungry almost every month of the year. And as we have witnessed lately Operation Hunger has done all in its power to raise the millions of rand needed to feed South Africa's starving people.

For its part the South African Government has over the years done its utmost to encourage the decentralization of industry from the major cities to the smaller towns and even to the homelands, and the result of this decentralization policy — despite that many disagree with it — is that, for example, I recently counted twenty new factories ranging from carpet manufacturing to panel-beating and spray-painting of cars in one small area of Bophuthatswana near the tribal town of Saulspoort. These factories and many others create hundreds of job opportunities for people who would otherwise go to bed hungry. The pace of this decentralization and development has at times been shamefully slow and haphazard; but it has taken place and I for one am thankful.

Yes, there is much to be done, very much more, before the dark ghosts of hunger, deprivation and misery are banished forever from the lives of our rural people.

Development of the rural people must take place from grassroots-level upward and not from the top downwards as is now the case. Again and again the western white man has made the unforgivable mistake of doing things back-to-front in South Africa — and in the rest of Africa — starting where he should end and ending where he should have started. He has persistently forgotten that in order to assist a third world people towards the mountains of development, you must know it is wrong to start by building space-age skyscrapers, computerised factories and London-type supermarkets out in the bush. One must first start by marshalling the traditional talents and skills of the grassroot-level people, encouraging them to weave mats and baskets, do beadwork and smelt metal in the traditional way to create toys and objets d'art for overseas tourists. In short, encourage cottage industries first before you plant large factories in the bundu.

Before thrusting an ultra-modern John Deer tractor into the hands of an unlettered black person you must first introduce that person to basic things, such as manually operated tungsten borehole drills, clay-and-sand cooking stoves, old style forges and furnaces and Archimedes screws for raising irrigation water from the local river. If you do not do this the people will have nothing to fall back on once their shiny new tractors break down or run out of diesel oil, and these people will remember your name with a curse and not with a sigh of gratitude.

In the last twenty years or so I have tried again and again to point out these important facts to organizations such as the then Bantu Investment Corporation[180] and the Urban Foundation,[181] but my well-meant advice was ignored and taken simply to be the mouthings of a crank and an idiot.

Today South Africa is swimming in blood, mostly black blood, and she is caught in a vicious spiral of endemic violence, because in this land there are many well-meaning whites who, though willing to help my people in many ways, regard the black as a brainless child not worth listening to.

Getting back to the homelands. The men who created the policy of separate development, men such as Doctor Hendrik Verwoerd, must have had a wonderful sense of humour, because in creating the various black homelands and national states they played a gigantic joke upon South African posterity in creating something they knew would perpetuate itself regardless of what changes would

154

be made in the government of the country and in government policy.

President PW Botha's Government has embarked upon an urgent reform programme and is doing away with some of the most deep-rooted and oldest discriminatory laws in the country; but we all know, we who live in South Africa and know its harsh realities, the reform programme will stop short of dismantling the homelands system because should the South African Government try to dismantle countries such as Transkei,[182] Ciskei,[183] Venda,[184] and Bophuthatswana[185] and incorporates them into the Republic of South Africa — what the West is demanding — it would meet with bitter resistance from the governments of those countries and many of their people.

And why do I say this? I say this because there are, firstly, thousands of men and women in the homelands who have become extremely wealthy and powerful as a result of the policy of separate development; men and women who would not willingly give up their wealth and power in the name of reform.

For example, in Bophuthatswana there is a tribe of people, numbering several hundred thousand souls, that enjoys a very high standard of living because a platinum mine — the largest in the Southern Hemisphere — stands in its territory. This tribe is the Bafokeng Tribe of Phokeng and it owns the great Rustenburg Platinum Mine. Before the creation of Bophuthatswana, these men and women were nothing but down-trodden peasants, who starved in the bush and eked out a living working for white farmers or as migrant labourers in the cities. Now they own schools, churches and comfortable houses, and they own cars, trucks and vans as a result of the royalties the mine is earning for them. Only bloody brute force would separate the Bafokeng people from their beloved "Platinamu Meyini."

I would advise those who dare to sneer at my words to recall the Katangese Succession[186] of the early Sixties and the many bloody battles that were fought over the Union Minier Copper Mines in that province of the country now called Zaire.

I have given you only one example; but there are many, many more. In the national states there are former schoolteachers, former policemen and former office clerks who are today saluted as government ministers and even as heads of state, and such people will never willingly climb down from their thrones of power and take the long downward sloping path to the mists of oblivion. People who have tasted freedom, no matter how false; and power, no matter how illusionary, never willingly give up such things; and nowhere on earth is this more forcibly true than in Africa. Let me ask you: Just how many African heads of state have you known who willingly and peacefully relinquished power? Precisely what do the many coups for which Africa has now become so famous mean to you?

I have said the men who created the homelands concept in South Africa were brilliant men who knew exactly what they were doing and I beg to say that again. Take a map of South Africa showing the various black homelands, and carefully study it. You shall quickly notice just how strangely and seemingly illogically fragmented some of these homelands are. You will notice for example that KwaZulu, in particular, consists of many tiny pieces, like a worm-devoured cowhide, and these pieces are spread over most of the province of Natal.

You will also notice that Lebowa, Gazankulu and Bophutha-tswana too are strangely fragmented and look like splashes of cowdung dropped across a rural dirt road by an ox with a running stomach. Many black homeland leaders have for years voiced their objections to this fragmentation, complaining that a country consisting of little bits and pieces is impossible to develop, let alone rule properly.

Some members of the official opposition in South Africa have gone on record over the years as saying that the very idea of these fragmented national states is "crazy"; and that the Government should "consolidate" them without delay. But one extremely amusing and revealing thing that has happened over the years is that the South African Government has been, to put it mildly, rather lukewarm in its efforts to consolidate these homelands, and I think I know the reason why.

Separate development was created by people who distrusted the black man and feared him, by people who wished to give the black African a semblance of freedom but not unity, and by people who, even while they spent millions in creating the national states — and even going so far as to give them flags and "independence" — were aware that these statelets might one day unite under some future black war-leader and try to topple white authority in South Africa.

There was no madness behind the creation of these fragmented "states," but rather cold logic born of distrust and fear. A rebellious state consisting of three or more pieces scattered over the face of your country is the easiest thing on earth to crush; you simply send your armies to surround each of the pieces, cut them off from each other and destroy them at leisure. In light of this it comes as no surprise that the most disgracefully fragmented homeland of all is KwaZulu, the land of the warlike Zulu people, whom the Afrikaners have distrusted and feared for a long time because of the long history of warfare between them and this proud warrior nation.

Despite all this, the homelands are now realities to reckon with in South Africa. They were created and they function, and cannot just be wished away.

28

Nelson Mandela

Please, do not fall into the trap of underestimating the depth of the violence gripping South Africa these days. Do not make the mistake that many politicians in South Africa and other parts of the world are making, which is to regard these bloody upheavals as mere political protest that would be brought to an end by "dismantling apartheid" or "negotiating with the genuine leaders of the black people" such as Nelson Rolihlahla Mandela.

I say by all means Nelson Mandela *must* be released from prison, released just as the South West African leader Herman Andimba Toivo-Ja-Toivo[187] has been released. Mandela must be released, UNCONDITIONALLY, if only as an act of compassion and as an act of calling the radical's bluff in South Africa.

For years now leftwing radicals have been spreading a lie throughout the world regarding Mandela. They tell us that if this old and ailing man is released, peace will come to South Africa. Only by releasing Mandela will this deadliest of falsehoods be exposed for the confidence trick and cheap lie that it is.

Mandela is regarded by thousands of young black people in South Africa as the spiritual leader of the ANC; but he enjoys little support and respect among the grassroots supporters of the Pan Africanist Congress[188] (PAC), which is the other revolutionary organization facing South Africa over the barrel of a gun nowadays, an organization that I regard as by far the deadliest terrorist organization ever seen in southern Africa.

And even if the impossible were ever to happen and a released Mandela succeeded in negotiating peace between South Africa and the ANC, the PAC would refuse to recognize that peace and take to the bush and start fighting, and moreover Mandela would immediately lose credibility and respect in the eyes of diehard ANC cadres. They would leave the ANC and go over to the PAC and join it with their weapons.

The ANC is a multi-racial organization, which is forced by its very character or its composition to avoid going all out in its terror campaign against South Africa. The PAC on the other hand is a black exclusivist organization that has no such scruples, and from its very inception it showed an extremism and aggressiveness hitherto unknown in an organization of this sort in South Africa.

The motto of the PAC is "Africa for the Africans" and it means exactly that. Africa for the black bantu speaking Africans; an Africa in which neither the coloureds, the whites or the Indians have any place.

If you look back into the history of the PAC you will notice two things, firstly, it was the first organization in South Africa to encourage the murder of white people as part of its policy. It had a group of panga-wielding assassins under it wing known as Poqo, which specialized in attacking and hacking white caravanners and holiday makers to death in the Eastern Cape. And where the leadership of the ANC used to project a sleek ultramodern and well-dressed image to the world at large, the leaders and founders of the PAC went out of their way to dress like poor rural Africans — usually in tattered khaki shirts, trousers, car-tyre sandals and tattered greatcoats.

One of the founder members of the PAC, Josias Madzunya,[189] was especially fond of dressing this way and he, together with others in the hierarchy of the organization, scoffed at the ANC's moderation and "elitism," selling their organization as a grassroots organization to which even the poorest of the poor blacks were welcome.

The whole of the Eastern Cape actually supports the PAC and not the ANC, and it should come as no surprise to you, therefore, that part of South Africa is characterized by unending township violence, by multiple murders of black moderate leaders and their families, by ruthless intimidation of people on a massive scale and by successful black boycotts of whites that have caused the collapse of many white businesses.

Any person who is concerned about the escalating conflict situation in South Africa, any person who wishes to see genuine peace come like a young bride to the troubled country of my forefathers, must not dare overlook the PAC and the deadly and disruptive part it could play in this country. And any thinking person who wants to see peace and reconciliation within his or her lifetime in South Africa, must call for the release of Nelson Mandela both for the reasons I have named and those I am yet to reveal.

No person must be under illusions that Mandela's release will take away the clouds of war and death hanging over South Africa. I knew Nelson Mandela, I knew him as a brilliant, handsome young Xhosa lawyer with gentle eyes and a soft voice, and although I abhor the organization he is the leader of, an organization which has thrice tried to end my earthly life, I know and can swear before, God that this man is not a man of violence, but rather a moderate man who was driven by intransigent and uncaring white men into violence and extremism.

But there is something I also know about this man, and it is that he can be dangerously altruistic and self-sacrificing, and he is a man of great courage . . . AND IT IS IN THIS THAT SOUTH AFRICA'S GREATEST DANGER LIES. Mandela knows, just as any observant and thinking black person who looks at things coldly and objectively knows, that over the years the true leadership of the ANC has slowly passed from the hands of the moderate "Old Guard" — to which Oliver Tambo belongs — into the hands of ruthless, highly trained and ambitious young militants who no longer believe in empty talk and time wasting negotiation; but who now rather have faith in the limpet mine, the hand-grenade and the AK-47.

These militants believe that they are winning the struggle for possession of South Africa, they see the whole world rapidly turning away from the South African Government and giving them and their organization support, both moral, diplomatic and financial. They are smelling blood and future victory and because of this they are pushing harder and fanning the flames of riot and carnage in the townships to white-heat, while at the same time becoming more and more aggressive in their bomb planting and landmine laying operations in the rural areas of South Africa.

These young militants are aware of one harsh fact of life in Africa, and it is that THE HAND THAT CARRIES THE GUN RULES THE LAND, and they will never really allow an old man, no matter how revered and charismatic, to come out of prison and steal their thunder, and rob them of the however remote chance of becoming rulers of a liberated South Africa one day.

Not very long ago the South African Government released Toivo-Ja-Toivo from prison after many years of pressure from the outside world, and there were those who naively believed that the release of this great man would bring peace to Namibia . . . . It did not because once released Toivo-Ja-Toivo found himself a man of the past, a spent force like an arrow which has spent its passion in a tree, and PRECISELY THE SAME FATE WOULD BEFALL NELSON MANDELA IF HE WERE EVER TO BE RELEASED.

Mandela has repeatedly refused offers of conditional release from prison, but some men jailed with him have accepted and have been freed. Mandela is an old and sick man, who obviously loves his family and misses them, so why does he persistently refuse being released? It takes great courage for a sick man like Mandela to do what he is doing, each day spent in prison must be great agony to him now. But why is he refusing? Why does he not want to be released.

I strongly suspect that Nelson Mandela wishes to die in prison, so as to become the greatest black martyr that Africa and the world has ever seen; and for a man of his courage and altruistic nature this is not at all far-fetched or as impossible as it may seem. MAKE NO MISTAKES: MANDELA'S DEATH IN PRISON WOULD BE THE GREATEST DISASTER EVER TO STRIKE SOUTH AFRICA. IT WOULD UNITE BLACKS ACROSS THE BROAD SPECTRUM OF CLASS, TRIBE AND EDUCATIONAL STANDARD, AND UNLEASH A BLOODY HOLOCAUST IN THIS LAND.

There are black leaders in southern Africa who I like to refer to as "double-status" leaders, in that they are not only powerful in the modern political sphere, but also command vast followings among the tradition-bound grassroots-level black peasantry as well. Cynics may scoff and skeptics may sneer, but black tradition is still a force to be reckoned with in southern Africa, and whoever is aware of this carries in his hands a golden key with which he could open a door to a shining future for the subcontinent. He also carries an iron key with which he could open the door that could lead the whole of the subcontinent into the very jaws of hell.

A double-status South African black leader is someone who is either a chief or a member of one of the many black royal families by birth and who, because of this, is respected and revered by thousands of people both within and outside the borders of the homelands to which he belongs or is the ruler of. But this leader also holds another important post, which is either that of head of state of his homeland or that of leader of a certain powerful modern political organization or movement.

Take for example Chief Mangosuthu Buthelezi. This leader is not only a chief commanding the love and loyalty of tens of thousands of Zulus both inside and outside Natal, but he is also the President of the Inkatha Movement, which is the most powerful modern political and cultural movement ever seen in southern Africa. NOW LET ME REVEAL TO YOU THAT LIKE CHIEF BUTHELEZI, NELSON MANDELA IS ALSO A DOUBLE-STATUS BLACK LEADER, WITH ONE FOOT IN THE MODERN POLITICAL WORLD AND THE OTHER FOOT IN THE BLACK TRADI-TIONAL WORLD, and the reason for this is that Mandela is a member by birth of one of the most ancient and powerful royal families in Transkei. He is respected by tens of thousands of Xhosa people in the Transkei as well as Ciskei, and should he die in prison thousands of such people would take up arms and fight, and they would fight and die by the thousands not because they understand or believe in the preachings of the ANC, but because, according to black tradition (all black tribes), if a prince or chief dies while held captive by an enemy tribe, it is an insult that must be cleansed by both our blood and that of the enemy tribe in whose captivity our prince or chief died.

Like the Zulus with whom they share a common origin, the Xhosas of Transkei and Ciskei are a fiercely royalist people and to them things such as the chieftainship are very sensitive subjects indeed.

Many years ago in the 1950s, the Nationalist Government of South Africa caused widespread hut-burnings and bloodshed in a part of the Transkei by unseating a popular tribal chief and forcing an unwanted chief upon the proud Pondo people. Scores of Pondos died in those disturbances, which took many months to quieten. Recently, the Government of Transkei had to move with great speed to avert a bloody catastrophe in that country, when the body of a very popular chief who had died in exile in Zambia was brought back by members of his family for burial in his home district. Thousands of people from all over South Africa had intended to converge upon the Transkei to attend the funeral of this chief who had also been a member of the ANC in the closing years of his life. Transkeian troops were called up, roadblocks were manned throughout the country and buses and other vehicles, trying to reach the territory of the dead man were turned away. The funeral was surrounded by a wall of military force and the dead chief's body was taken out of the mortuary and buried by soldiers, much against the wishes of the family.

By remaining in prison Nelson Mandela poses the greatest single threat to the peace and security of South Africa. He holds a sword to South Africa's throat and he knows it. He is achieving far more behind bars than he would if he were a free man far beyond the walls of Pollsmoor Prison. [190]

If he were ever to die he would become a powerful hero-saviour in the eyes of black militants and radicals, and a shining martyr in the eyes of thousands of tradition-bound black men and women. He would be the greatest hero-saviour in the troubled history of the South African black people.

News of his death in prison would reverberate from one end of the world to the other, for he is the most talked about political prisoner alive. Mandela's death would cause protest marches and violence in other western countries besides South Africa, and there would be race riots not only in Great Britain but also in the USA.

I cannot for the life of me understand why a man of PW Botha's vision and understanding fails to realize the danger posed by the continuing imprisonment of Nelson Mandela. I cannot understand why a man such as President Botha who has risked all to reform South Africa, a thing which was unthinkable not so long ago, should at the same time be making the deadly mistake of playing into the hands of black radicalism by keeping Mandela locked up, and by placing impossible conditions, such as publicly renouncing violence, in front of the imprisoned man as prerequisites for his release.

Surely every thinking person in South Africa knows that were Mandela ever to accept President Botha's conditions for his release, he would be a dead man the moment he walked out of that prison; and his murderers would be the very radicals and militants who had been bowing to his memory only a short while before. It would not be the first time in human history that an angry people has turned upon its god and killed him when it found that behind all that halo, glitter and shining majesty, he was nothing but a trembling, scaly little demon.

I say again, it is in South Africa's deepest interests that Nelson Mandela be freed from prison. More I cannot say. South Africa is already in deep, deadly danger, and all that which is evil, which was destined to happen, has already happened to this country, and the duty of those who love South Africa now have to act to lessen the danger this country finds itself in, even to the extent of letting Mandela and his fellow prisoners go free.

South Africa faces armed revolutionaries now and can no longer afford the luxury of wasting time and effort upon men and women from the misty shores of yesterday. South Africans, are even now blissfully unaware of the nature and the full extent of the danger that faces them.

29

South Africa's Isolation and Sanctions

People who have decided to disinvest from South Africa, people who have decided to isolate this country and punish her with sanctions, are people who have not learned the lessons from recent history. Isolating South Africa is the last thing the West should ever consider doing.

After the Armistice of 1918 Germany[191] was isolated and ostracized by many European nations; humiliation and insult were heaped upon her and her people began to suffer in their thousands. Her money became useless and her economy collapsed, and her once-great industries became but ghosts of their once mighty selves.

But then came the Nazis under Adolf Hitler, who promised the German people a restoration of German greatness, prosperity and soaring national pride. Hitler screamed and ranted, roared and raved, and the mesmerized crowds bellowed their approval like excited cattle after a rainstorm at the end of a long draught. Within the space of a few years The Third Reich[192] was born to the sound of trumpets, of thousands cheering and of many booted feet marching in the cobbled streets of re-born German cities. Germany sold her soul to the devil behind the stifling curtain of isolation that the European powers had placed between themselves and her, and the rest is all-too-familiar history and needs no repeating here.

But let me say this, had Germany been forgiven and embraced, instead of being humiliated and rejected, things such as the

Holocaust would never have occurred, and the Second World War would never have broken out.

When Israel came into being, just after the Second World War, the neighbouring Arab nations did their utmost to try and strangle her at birth. They greeted her with violence, with angry words and with ringing curses, forcing her to lash back and fight fiercely for survival. The Arabs doubled their efforts, becoming more shrill-voiced and angry, and then they tried to kill Israel by simply ignoring her as if she did not exist. But again they failed and Israel grew from strength to strength like an unwanted child.

Smarting under rejection, injury and humiliation, Israel soon adopted an extremely aggressive stance towards her neighbours; she locked horns with them and defeated them, singly or in groups, again and yet again, growing ever stronger and becoming more determined to survive and fight after each bloody encounter. One day the world heard whispers to the effect that the tiny state, no bigger than South Africa's largest game reserve, the Kruger National Park, now possessed a fearsome arsenal of nuclear weapons. The Arabs were shaken and they still are to this very day.

Israel now dominates the whole of the Middle East like a fire-breathing dragon and there is nothing that the poor Arabs can do to make her vanish and go away — although no doubt they will still continue to try. Had they not greeted her with isolation, rejection and enmity, had they tried to reach some kind of under-standing and accommodation with her earlier on, the Arab nations would have gained a gentle-eyed friend and neighbour instead of a fearsome enemy.

Isolating an unwanted nation only makes it much stronger and more determined to survive and prosper. Also isolating and rejecting a nation because one happens to disagree with the way it does certain things opens the way for raving extremists to come to power. Within a short space of time you find yourself confronted with aggressive people with whom you can no longer reason . . . people who will put out their tongues at you, hiss like puff-adders at you and tell you to go straight to Hell.

I would like to show you yet two more examples of the danger of ostracizing a nation with whose policies you happen not to agree. Listen please: In 1948 civil war broke out in China between the Nationalists led by Chiang Kai-Shek[193] and the Communists led by Mao Tse-tung. The war was really a final, devastating conflict between two sides that had been exchanging blows since the 1930s. As fate would have it, it was Mao Tse-tung who won and Chiang Kai-Shek fled with his surviving warlords and remaining armies to the small island of Formosa, which was soon renamed Taiwan.

When the West, the Americans especially, saw that the side that they had supported had crumbled and that the Communists were now in power in Peking they reacted with typical stupidity and short-sightedness. They decided to isolate Communist China and to treat her as if she did not exist and even went so far as to refer to Taiwan as the Republic of China, which was ridiculous in the extreme. They repeated the same mistake that they had made regarding Germany many years before, proving to the world that they were incapable of heeding the harsh lessons of history.

A dark screen of isolation fell all around China and for some time there was a dark and sinister silence from behind the screen. And then China struck, suddenly and violently in a way that the West had not expected. Her forces swept into Tibet, that sacred land of great monasteries and unrevealed mysteries, and they took it with negligible resistance from the time-hazy and peaceful Tibetans. The great priest of Tibet, the Dalai Lama,[194] was forced to flee from his snowbound native land to seek shelter in the land of strangers.

The horrified West watched helplessly, unable to lift a finger to assist the enslaved people of Tibet. And then war broke out in Korea, and the Americans and their allies rallied to the United Nations flag and entered the war. Little did they consider that the whole thing could be a cleverly-laid Chinese trap in which the North Koreans were little more than bait, cheese with which to catch the star-spangled mouse.

The thunder of battle filled the icy hills and the snow-covered valleys of the Korean peninsular, first to the one side and then to the other went the fickle fortunes of war until at last the Allies got the upper hand and drove the shattered and demoralized North Koreans helter-skelter up the length of the peninsular towards the Yalu River, which forms the northernmost border between Korea and China.

It was then that the Chinese stormed into the war in a fearsome, howling flood of humanity that overwhelmed the United Nations forces and pushed them back, back down the peninsular towards the sea. A cease-fire was arranged and peace talks soon began af-

169

ter the strange war had reached some kind of stalemate, and the war ended with an armistice of some kind . . . .

A few years after this the world was shaken by newsreports that China had exploded an atomic bomb in the centre of one of her immeasurably vast plains. This report was immediately followed by another, to the effect that China now had a hydrogen bomb and was rapidly building up a powerful arsenal of such weapons. It was not long after this that China emerged from her isolation to help two African countries, Tanzania and Zambia, in the building and financing of the Tanzam Railway, a thing that European nations said was impossible and would, in any case, be extremely expensive to build.

By going in where other countries had feared to tread, the Chinese impressed millions of Africans throughout Africa and won the undying gratitude and friendship of many black-ruled African states. China then went on to test a huge ballistic missile capable of carrying an atomic warhead across the Pacific Ocean, revealing for the first time that she now had the ability to rain nuclear death upon the Soviets, the Americans or any other country or groups of countries that dared try something with her.

Just after the end of the Second World War the tyrant of the Soviet Union, Joseph Stalin, provoked the West to bitter anger by blockading Berlin, and also by saying many things and doing many things that proved to his former allies in the war against Hitler that he was about to step into the dead German's shoes and threaten the whole of the human race with yet another World War.

As a result of the battering received by both the Soviet Union and the West during the Second World War neither had the will nor the strength to go to war once more. They elected to place a dark and angry barrier between them while they hastily rebuilt their shattered economies, ruined cities and disrupted industries, and regrouped their armies and rearmed them.

The West had confidence that massive as the Russian armies were, it could deal with them if they attacked because at the time only America possessed atomic weapons. The Soviet Union strengthened the material and psychological Iron Curtain that it had placed around itself and those European countries it had gobbled up and enslaved during the war. Russia built and greatly strengthened the infamous Berlin Wall, making it the cruellest and most sophisticated man-trap in human history, and then it enlisted the services of spies and turncoats to ferret out American atomic-bomb secrets, and acquired them with laughable ease.

In 1956 the Hungarian people revolted, seeking to rid themselves of Russian oppression and exploitation once and for all and bloody violence erupted in the streets of Budapest. For a few heady weeks, for an all to brief a space of time, the Hungarians savoured the wine of freedom and drank deep and long. But the paradise did not last, the wild joy was doomed to fade away into screams of agony and terror as the Russians unleashed their fearsome military might and smothered the Hungarians under a creeping blanket of hundreds of tanks, guns and thousands of soldiers.

The Hungarian revolution crumbled and thousands of Hungarians fled from their native land never to return, leaving uncounted thousands dead in the shell-pitted streets.

Some years went by and then a second Russian-dominated nation tried to rebel but was crushed just as quickly and as pitilessly as Hungary had been years before. That nation was Czechoslovakia, a nation of hardworking people who supplied the Russians with heavy trucks, excavators and other machinery. Again the West watched with folded arms, unable to do anything whatsoever, while the Russians battered the Czechs into submission.

But the story was different some three years ago, when the Polish people led by an aggressive little trade-unionist named Lec Walesa thumbed their noses at the Russians and stuck out their tongues at the Polish Government in the full glare of the spotlight of world attention and sympathy, because now there was no barrier of isolation behind which the Soviets could massacre and enslave with impunity.

What I am trying to tell you is that tyranny thrives and extremism flourishes within its borders once a country has been isolated and ostracized by the other countries around it, and that far from weakening under the weight of boycotts and sanctions the country tends to flourish and even tends to end up having acquired atomic weapons. And those who do not wish to see a proliferation of nuclear weapons amongst the smaller countries of the world should vigorously oppose those who preach the isolation and ostracizing of South Africa and her people.

There is suspicion that South Africa possesses a small nuclear arsenal, and I am one who believes that such an arsenal does indeed exist, because South Africa has in many other ways followed in the footsteps of Israel, Communist China, Germany and Russia, and has reacted to attempts at isolating her in precisely the same ways in which those countries reacted.

Today South Africa, like Israel and Communist China before her, has adopted a very aggressive posture in both the diplomatic and military spheres towards her neighbouring countries and towards the world at large. With incredible "chutzpah"[195] she has managed to break the long-standing arms boycott by somehow acquiring the most modern weapons' technology from countries such as Canada where she obtained the assistance of a weapons-manufacturing concern in creating her ultra-modern G2 long-range cannon. South Africa has found ways around sports boycotts and things such as the Gleneagles Agreement.[196]

People who wish to see apartheid continue and flourish, people who want to see escalating conflict in the subcontinent and people who want to see an extremist ultra-rightwing dictatorship come to power in South Africa within the next two years, should fight for South Africa's isolation.

But people who want to see the end of violence in South Africa, who want to see men such as Mandela released from prison, and people who want to see reconciliation between black and white as well as flowering peace and green prosperity in South Africa, should resist all attempts to isolate my fatherland.

I want to issue a word of warning to countries such as the USA and Great Britain: Please be careful of how you handle the South African issue because should you make mistakes and bring about a racial upheaval in this country your own countries too would be engulfed by the ripple-effects. I say this because I have been to Great Britain and lived for a number of months in the United States and have personal knowledge of the tensions that exist between black people and white people in those countries.

And finally let me give a reply to those unmitigated cretins, those ranting idiots, who are calling for the total withdrawal of American investments from South Africa and the closing down of American firms. My reply shall be in two parts, and the first part shall be the following little story:

I want you to imagine a mighty aircraft, a great Boeing 747, flying high in the flawless heavens, coming from we know not where and bound for we know not what distant land. All is well aboard the great aircraft, all is at peace. The passengers are relaxing in their seats, some dozing, some reading books and magazines, some scribbling furiously upon note-pads and some talking animatedly. The air-hostess appears at the far end of the passenger deck pushing a trolley in front of her and preparing to serve meals to the passengers.

All of a sudden two of the passengers leap to their feet with loud lunatic shouts, one of them clutching a handgrenade and the other brandishing an automatic pistol. The passengers are warned to "shut up" and sit very still if they value their lives because "this is a hijack." The leading hijacker walks towards the control-cabin with the grenade while the second hijacker stands in the middle of the passenger deck with his back to the rear of the Boeing. The air-hostess sees the leading hijacker coming towards her and her eyes widen with fear and surprise.

Then a man appears at the rear of the aircraft, emerging from one of the toilets, and for a few moments surveys the scene. The man is tall, strikingly handsome with thick dark hair, deep-set eyes, an aquiline nose and a hard, thin-lipped mouth. It is obvious that this man is a typical hero, a lover and rescuer of beautiful women and killer of hooligans, and a real rip-roaring Rambo-type.

He springs into action, launching himself across the space that separates him from the second hijacker, like a hungry lion springing upon an impala. Hero and hooligan go down in a welter of arms and legs. The hooligan's neck is broken and the gun ripped out of his villainous hand. The leading hijacker, alerted by the disturbance behind him, whirls around and stares with bulging, drug-crazed eyes at the gun now rock-steady in the hero's hand. "Wha . . . ?" he babbles.

The hero fires, three thunderous reports blending into one monstrous sound, and the hijacker is sent flying backwards by the impact of the bullets to fall with a crash against the hostess's food-trolley. As the lifeless body falls, the grenade explodes, blowing a fearful hole in the side of the aircraft. Screaming passengers, papers and other items are sucked through the hold by the fearful decompression and the great jet staggers briefly like a stricken eagle in the heavens before diving nose-first towards the ocean far below — trailing bits of twisted metal and other debris as well as broken human bodies like a hideous comet's tail behind it.

Now please tell me, will the dead passengers thank the equally dead hero when they meet him in the Hereafter? Will they thank him for rescuing them from the two hijackers? I think not; I think they will pick up ghostly sticks and heavenly stones and shower him with them, and pursue him down the slippery slope to Hell where a smiling Devil stands with folded arms at the fiery entrance, waiting happily.

People who are campaigning for total disinvestment and for laws that will force the remaining American firms to close down and withdraw their money from South Africa are like the foolish hero in the incident I have just described. They foolishly do and suggest things that would result in the death of thousands of our people in South Africa.

Like mad witchdoctors in one Zulu fable, they believe that the best way to rid a man of a chronic headache is to lift up a heavy flat stone and brain him with it, telling the world that you are only killing the Pain-Spirit and thus freeing the patient from agony in future.

As a result of disinvestment and sanctions, unemployment on an unprecedented scale will result with hundreds of people queueing in front of firms and other places of employment, waiting for jobs that are no longer to be had. After this will come starvation on a scale far worse than that in Ethiopia, with tens of thousands of black children dying of hunger, kwashiorkor and other nutrition-related diseases. There would be savage outbreaks of rioting over food, and in the rural parts of the country starving people might resort to cannibalism in order to survive.

It is people who have led soft, sheltered and pampered lives, people who have never known what it feels like to go to bed hungry, people who have never known the heart-rending sight of a child dying of kwashiorkor — its belly distended, its limbs as thin as dried sticks, its mouth mindlessly open and its staring eyes empty and haunted by flies — who are calling for sanctions. I have seen such starving sights Heaven knows how many times in southern Africa and I do not wish to see them again.

As a result of all-out sanctions and trade boycotts our people would die in far larger numbers than the Ethiopians died and there would be no golden-haired Bob Geldoff[197] and his shining singers to come to our aid. The black people would die like flies BUT THE WHITE PEOPLE WOULD SURVIVE: they would survive because unlike the blacks, they are able to save some of the money they earn, whereas the pay-packets of most black people are shared with unemployed relatives who the working black is compelled, by tradition, to live with and support.

And in our townships there are working people who have as many as ten relatives who they support, and who range in age from elderly people in their seventies or sixties right down to babies of two years old or even less. I personally support sixteen relatives and of these, three are in Natal.

American firms must not be forced out of South Africa, nor must they agree to be forced out by dreamy-eyed and mischief-mongering lunatics because these firms have done much in the last twenty years to make the lot of the black man easy in South Africa. They have built, or helped to build, schools such as the beautiful Pace College[198] in Soweto. They were the first to introduce promotion on merit for employees so that it became possible for a black to hold a very high position, a position which in the past would have been held by a white in the days of job reservation.

There is not a single seriously workseeking black person in our townships who does not dream of one day finding a job with the Coca-Cola company, IBM, Anglo-American and other firms associated with America, in one way or another. These are secure, prestige jobs where you are made to feel like a human being with dignity and not simply as a number at the clocking-in cubicle and a nameless face at the workfloor.

In the homes of black people that I know, the question of sanctions is a topic of urgent and fearful discussion. Don't people in America realize we are going to starve to death? Why do they not realize that the death of apartheid can be brought about by rapid upliftment of the black people, not actions that threaten to deprive us.

30

Conclusion

I call on all thinking people to be aware that our country's problem is not a political one, but rather a *human* problem, and that by trying to solve it by political means alone is going to end in failure and in tragedy. I want to point out one thing — without understanding, without full, frank, and open communication between black and white in South Africa, no amount of reform will ever meet with any success.

It is most essential that the black and white people of South Africa go on a "Great Trek" of the spirit, and discover each other anew. All stereotypes must be thrown overboard, all generalizations must be done away with, and South Africa's races must stand together and shake hands under the light of the sun that is Almighty God.

South Africa is faced with a great tragedy — let no-one underestimate this, let no-one seek to play down this awful fact — that if disaster is allowed to engulf our country, that disaster will overflow into other countries. I cannot stress this enough. It would only need a little spark to ignite a conflagration that would swallow not only South Africa, but also much of Great Britain, and the USA.

My country is sick and it needs help; the help of true physicians in its hour of illness. We do not require quacks. We do not required know-it-alls who jet in on wings of flame from far countries such as the United States; who stay in my country for a short, enchanted visit, enjoying our country's hospitality doing indifferent research into our country's problems — and then returning to their native land where they skulk behind desks to either recommend sanctions or write a lot of drivel about South Africa, such as the book that I have recently read by Mr Joseph Lelyveld.

I want it to be known that we have no time in South Africa for cynics who use my country as a scapegoat and as a cover to hide their own grievous transgressions.

OUR COUNTRY NEEDS HELP.

Our country has cried out for assistance, and that assistance should be in the form of understanding, of contact and communication, and not in the form of ostracism, condemnation, and vilification.

What is happening to South Africa is something that is happening to many countries throughout the world. What is happening to my country is part of a disease that is spreading from continent to continent, across the face of our planet. It is a disease that must be tackled calmly, honestly, and frankly by all people who wish to see mankind survive upon this globe.

I say to you all that South Africa must not be allowed to die. South Africa must live. South Africa must survive. South Africa must prosper.

She must not be shackled with the chains of punitive sanctions, placed upon her wrists and ankles by cynics, who really do not care one damned bit about the welfare of her people. I cannot understand why men like Archbishop Desmond Tutu,[199] why men like Teddy Kennedy[200] should call for sanctions against my country. I wish to ask these two gentlemen, as well as all the others who have contributed towards the sanctions that have been forced onto my country:

DO YOU REALIZE WHAT YOU ARE DOING?

How can you, on the one hand, claim to be Christian God-fearing people and on the other be willing to destroy an entire country? Dare you stand one day before the vast audience-chamber of human history, and say to men of the future and women of years to come, that you were people of justice? Do you really think that by punishing South Africa with sanctions you are going to solve our problem for us? If so, you are politically naive, as well as dangerously misguided and stupid.

I have the deepest respect and admiration for the great nation of the United States. I admire the American people of all races for their great achievements and for their leadership of the world in many fields; but there is one thing that I do not understand about the people of this great country. The Americans seem incapable of learning from the harsh university of human experience; they tend to repeat the same mistakes that they made before, again and yet again. I cannot understand in the name of my ancestors why they do this.

The Americans are past masters at embracing lost causes. They are past masters of adopting the wrong cause at the expense of the right one. For example: They stood and watched while Haile Selassie[201] was deposed and destroyed, leaving the stage open for a bloody-handed tyrant named Mengistu Haile Mariam,[202] who is buying champagne while the Ethiopian people are dying like flies.

And some of these Americans, to their eternal shame, cheered and ululated like wedding-guests at a chieftain's wedding when Mohammed Reza Shah,[203] the Shah of Iran, was overthrown. They cheered when that dying man suffered exile, humiliation, and finally a lonely death upon some unchartered island.

And look at the beast that has hatched in the Land of Patience. Look at the Ayatollah Khomeini[204] and see what he is doing. And if my memory serves me correctly; during the rule of President Jimmy Carter,[205] a US strike force tried to invade Iran to rescue hostages held there and failed dismally. I beg that this great nation of America should set its sights right and act as the guardian and the protector of the free world.

She must play her rightful role as the leader of mankind. America must stop being a contradiction within a contradiction. She must be an upholder of liberty, to be feared, admired and respected by all of us. She should not bring about the destruction of helpless people — people who she is unable to help afterwards.

Why does America constantly work against her own interests? I cannot understand it. I cannot understand why this world is like a madman whose mind is split in two. I cannot understand why this world has got such a twisted sense of justice. That it is well and proper for the USA to invade Libya with screaming F-15 fighter-jets, to bomb Libya and destroy the nests of terrorism in that country, and yet why it is *wrong* when South Africa retaliates against her landmine-planting enemies by destroying ANC bases in neighbouring countries.

Tell me, is evil less evil, or more evil, because it happens in a particular country which you either like or dislike?

Is wrong right, and right wrong, simply because it happens to people you love or dislike?

I cannot understand that wrong can be right, and right can be wrong. Just as I cannot understand why men who profess to be the children and followers of Jesus Christ — the reverend men and women of the World Council of Churches (WCC),[206] the men and the women who should be working for peace throughout this troubled world of ours — are the same people supporting terrorism.

Can you, being a healer of people, support murder and rapine on the other hand?

Can you, being a bringer of life, at the same time support death?

Can you be a sangoma and a sorcerer at the same time?

Jesus Christ was one thing, and one thing only: a Bringer of Light — he never ever condemned people to Hell or to die of starvation.

At no time did Jesus Christ urge the use of the sword upon the weak, the defenceless, and the innocent.

Even when He was about to be seized and taken away to a shameful death, the Son of God forbade Peter the fisherman from using his sword in defence of his Master.

He repudiated and rebuked him very sternly, saying, "Oh Peter, those who live by the sword, shall surely perish by it."

By doing so, Jesus Christ proved His oneness, His wholeness, and His consistency in the service of His God.

I cannot understand people who will dress a wound with the one hand, and then rip it open with the sword in the other.

I call upon the World Council of Churches to re-examine it's conscience under God.

I am not saying that the WCC should turn a blind eye to wrong, but I am saying that the WCC should not join hands with murderers and killers of the innocent, because that is not service to God. That is polluting God's name, and turning into a dirty lie every word that lies written within the pages of the Bible.

Mr Neil Kinnock[207] of the Labour Party in Great Britain is quoted as having said to Mrs Margaret Thatcher[208] on the issue of punitive sanctions against my country, that all that is required for the triumph of evil, is that the good people do nothing.

Are these the same kind of good people that are funding and supporting the WCC, I wonder.

If South Africa's reform initiative is going to have any credibility, it must go hand in hand with sound human relations and in order to create sound human relations; all actions and attitudes that bedevil and pollute this extremely important thing, on any individual's or group's part, must be identified and eliminated.

As a first step to the valleys of reform RACISM by all sections of South Africa's population — black, white, brown or yellow — must be OUTLAWED, and AT ONCE.

I want to call upon the South African Medical and Dental Council and other bodies in charge of medical personnel in South Africa to come out into the open and stop skulking behind the South African Government and initiate reforms of your own within the medical sphere and among the ranks of the doctors, nurses and paramedical personnel throughout this land. I want to tell this Association, just as I am telling the South African Government, the ANC, the financial institutions, and other bodies and organizations throughout this country this: You too are responsible for the slow dying of my native land, and as I am calling to you now — REFORM, MEND YOUR WAYS AND STOP PLAYING JEHOVAH WITH THE LIVES OF MY PEOPLE. IMPROVE RELATIONS BETWEEN DOCTORS, NURSES AND OTHER MEDICAL PEOPLE AND PATIENTS AND STAMP OUT DISEASES SUCH AS TUBERCULOSIS IN SOUTH AFRICA!

I further want to remind you that after the Second World War, doctors were hanged as war criminals in Germany; they were hanged for cruel and inhuman conduct towards patients, for abuse of their position as physicians. Beware that a similar fate does not overtake some of you one sunny day!

I feel nothing but cold hatred and contempt for those so-called black leaders who are urging our people along the path of violence and death, and I want to ask these supposed leaders these questions, if I may: Do you want South Africa to become another LEBANON? Have you asked the people of the near future — the people who will walk the plains of this country long after you are dead and gone, whether they will approve of the hatred and racial violence that your irresponsible actions and words of today are going to hand down to them? If a man comes to you troubled by impotence do you prescribe castration as the cure? If a woman comes to you with migraine would you prescribe a spoonful of cyanide and glass of water before she goes to bed at night? You are urging

181

our people to "necklace" others, have you read the story of Robespierre[209] who was guillotined by the very people he had been encouraging to guillotine others only a year before his screaming, cowardly death? Do YOU have the courage to die the death you so smilingly prescribe for others?

I call upon you all to follow the examples of MOSES and of MAHATMA GANDHI,[210] if you are the leaders that you claim to be, I challenge you to read books on history, where you shall find that leaders who led their people along the path of peace achieved much more than those who led their people along the path of war. Before you set your country on fire, accept the challenge I throw at your feet!

Let me say here and now that people who, through irresponsible utterances and reckless deeds, are encouraging the spread of the present unrest in black townships in South Africa are actually dooming us who live in the subcontinent to a war without end.

And now, I want to say something to MR OLIVER TAMBO the President of the African National Congress. I want you to immediately issue a directive ordering your cadres and activists everywhere in South Africa to cease, and to cease at once, their habit of burning people alive with car tyres. I further challenge the United Democratic Front to issue a similar directive to its zealots and activists throughout South Africa to stop, and to stop immediately, their habit of committing atrocities on defenceless black civilians. I, CREDO VUSAMAZULU ka FANA MUTHWA, am a sanusi and as such I am sworn to defend the sacred traditions and the Great Belief of my people to the grave and beyond it if need be, and I accuse the ANC and the UDF of sacrilegious conduct against the laws, traditions and gods of Africa.

I warn these organizations before the judgement seat of the Great Father, that if they do not immediately cease burning my people, I shall lead a religious crusade against them and all they stand for, even if I lose my life in doing so. If they make the mistake of taking my words as mere empty bluff, I challenge them to call that bluff and see. I further appeal to all God-fearing men and women throughout Africa and the world at large to distance themselves from these two organizations until they have publicly complied with my demand in writing, namely that all atrocities against unarmed civilians shall forthwith cease and all sacrilegious acts shall be ended.

I want to further remind OLIVER TAMBO that traditional beliefs are still a force to be reckoned with in southern Africa, which is why countries such as Zimbabwe have recognized the black traditional healer. I further wish to remind him that he belongs to one of the oldest and most revered families in the land of the Xhosa people, a family whose members, never once through the long years of Xhosa history, dirtied the sacred name of TAMBO with disgraceful actions and sacrilegious deeds. I further wish to remind him that even the most hardened communists respect religion. For example: President Saddam Hussein,[211] though a communist, respects the Islamic religion and realizes its value in holding his people together.

Colonel Muammar al-Qaddafi of Libya respects the Islamic religion and never once has he persecuted its followers, absolute dictator though he be. In Vietnam, Kampuchea (formely Cambodia) and Communist China, Buddhism is respected, and I demand that the ANC also give due respect to our traditional religion.

I wish to throw down my gauntlet at the feet of the Archbishop of Cape Town and head of the Anglican Church in South Africa, the Most Reverend Desmond Tutu, and other bishops, priests and laymen of all Christian churches in southern Africa. Stand up and be counted and lead a mass spiritual reform among the different races in southern Africa. I say it is wrong and immoral for reform in South Africa to be of only a POLITICAL NATURE as the case is now, and I say that this political reform will fail disastrously unless it is accompanied by spiritual reform by all people living on the southern tip of Africa.

I say the respected Anglican Archbishop is aware, just as I am aware, of just how cruel black people are towards each other in the course of their daily existence in the cities and townships. He is aware, just as I am aware, that on August 26, 1984 the "Extra" edition of the Sunday Times reported the police public relations officer, Major Joel Zwane, as saying there were literally thousands of wanted murderers at large in Soweto, and that during the period from 1982 to 1983 an incredible total of 2,475 people were murdered in this area alone. And, all these were "ordinary" street murders and not politically-inspired. Since that time the number of deaths has probably doubled or trebled, REVEALING THAT THERE IS SOMETHING SPIRITUALLY WRONG WITH THE PEOPLE OF SOWETO AND THE TOWNSHIPS IN SOUTH AFRICA, SOMETHING FOR WHICH THE WHITE MAN CANNOT BE

CONVENIENTLY BLAMED, AS IS ALWAYS THE CASE WHEN THINGS GO WRONG IN THE BLACK COMMUNITIES: "BLAME THE WHITE MAN AND HIS SYSTEM."

It is not the white man who says that a gang of thugs in Soweto should first rape a girl or a woman, and then murder her in cold blood for fear that she will identify them. It is not the white man who says that a gang of thugs should hack a helpless old man to pieces with machetes after they have picked his pockets. Nor is it the white man who says that a young footballer should be stabbed to death while escorting his blind grandmother to collect her pension, simply because he refused to play for the team his murderers support. It is not the law of the white man that says a young man has to have his face burned off with acid simply because he wears better clothes than his assailants; nor is it the white man who says that I should kill the man who the boss loves to send to the cafe to buy him sandwiches and cigarettes.

In my long stay in Soweto, I witnessed murders committed for no other motive than pure pleasure; and very often these were the most gruesome murders, with the victim's motionless body covered from head to foot with gaping, hideous wounds, some of which had obviously been inflicted upon the victim long after he or she had died. I have also seen many so-called "ritual" murders — the type of murder for which whites love to blame "witchdoctors," when it is sorcerers who commit this type of killing — and in these murders the corpse is always horribly mutilated with eyes, hands, liver and genitals missing. I know that these killings are often done on behalf of educated and extremely wealthy business people, who pay the killer or killers thousands for those parts of the corpse, which are dried, ground and afterwards added to magical mixtures and stored in the horns of slaughtered bulls . . . to bring good luck to the businessman or woman and so increase his or her bank balance.

The black man was not always so heartless, so unfeeling towards his own kind, because in olden days he was restrained by his traditional religion and later by the Christian religion, against such bloodthirsty cruelty, but it seems that over the years the bonds of religion have loosened in the soul of the black African just as his respect for and confidence in the laws of the State have disappeared altogether.

So, here is the first important field of activity I challenge Archbishop Tutu and other revered men of the cloth in South Africa to address their energies to: THE BLACK MAN MUST BE BROUGHT BACK TO GOD, HE MUST BE MADE ONCE MORE TO RESPECT THE SANCTITY OF HUMAN LIFE; TO ONCE MORE LOVE HIS NEIGHBOUR EVEN AS HE LOVES HIMSELF.

I would suggest to the Archbishop and other leaders of the church in South Africa that they draw up a charter setting out the guidelines for the proper treatment of people of all races in all financial institutions, hospitals, clinics, police-stations and other places to which people go for assistance. The Archbishop must then call upon all the leaders of these institutions to come to a public place to sign this charter as part of the great reform initiative in South Africa.

The Archbishop, and the South African Council of Churches,[212] should also seriously consider doing one important thing the South African Government appears to be either unwilling or unable to do, namely to appoint a watchdog committee whose aim would be to monitor the activities of black civic authorities with the view to putting an end to irregular practices, and also with the view of giving the township residents a dignified and trustworthy forum backed by the dignity of the Church in which to air their grievances without fear of reprisals from any quarter.

One of the root causes of the violence we see in our townships is that township residents are denied an outlet — a neutral outlet that has no connection whatsoever with the State — to air their grievances. A man, for example, who finds himself being forced out of his house through the machinations of a corrupt councillor or township manager, has no one to appeal to . . . especially if he is poor and cannot afford lawyer's fees. In short, I am calling upon the CHURCH in South Africa to perform vitally needed functions, most especially in the field of interracial relations, civic-authority and denizen relations.

The Church is in a far better position to save South Africa than the State is, because the Church, in the form of all the established churches and also in the form of the many religious sects with which the townships abound, has strong spiritual links with large sections of the black population. It enjoys absolute trust and can therefore play a positive role in healing rifts and cooling passions. In doing this the Church would not be dabbling in politics and would only be playing its historic role in southern Africa, a role it played with great success in the past, especially in the last century.

I am not a Christian any more and never shall be again, but I want to say this in all earnest, the best weapon against an evil philosophy is the good philosophy at your immediate disposal, and the only effective weapon South African has at the present against the communist menace, is religion. The Christian religion, the Islamic Religion and the Hindu religion as well as the Judaic religion, must be brought forward to play a dramatic and positive, as well as visible and creative, role in this country. The fate of South Africa is too important to be left in the hands of strait-jacketed and benighted politicians who see no further than the next election. MEN OF GOD MUST STAND FORTH NOW AND ACT.

The Church must assist the white man to reform, but it must also pressure the black man into reforming too. The black man must accept that he too is responsible for the mess that South Africa is in. He has never been honest with the white man in many ways and has again and again spoken one thing while thinking another. He has, for decades, caused the white man to make serious mistakes in those things that the white man was creating for the black's own benefit, by simply not telling the white man the full truth.

It is a truth known to all who are black, that deep in our hearts of hearts we prefer a one-party state and not a two-party democracy with a governing party and an opposition. We are rabid tribalists at heart, but we tell the world that we are anything but that and that tribalism is an ugly, outdated thing that has no place in the new Africa. Yet, when plum jobs open in our newly-independent country, we see to it that they get filled with members of our particular tribe. The black man has been a racist for decades, but he hides that fact from the world outside and is content to let the Afrikaner alone face the flak.

I cannot, and I will not, allow my country to drown in the flames of war, and I call upon all men who have taken on the mantles of leadership in our country to do their utmost to help prevent such a war from coming to South Africa. I further call upon President PW Botha, Mr Jaap Marais[213] as well as Mr Eugene Terre'Blanche[214] to show wisdom and do likewise or else face the contempt and the harsh judgement of future generations of South Africans.

I wish most especially to say this to Mr Terre'Blanche, leader of the Afrikaner Weerstandsbeweging: Sir, I have warned Oliver Tambo and now I am warning you. Please put away your ridiculous flags and command your stormvolke[215] warriors to go back to their father's farms. This is not the way to serve the interests of the great Afrikaner nation to which you and they belong. All this troglodyte[216] thuggery and Neanderthal violence on the part of your followers is doing incalculable harm to the Afrikaner people at an extremely critical time, and I appeal to you to put an end to it. South Africa, no matter how strong and militarily prepared she may be, would never survive a race-war, NO COUNTRY ON EARTH CAN, NOT EVEN NUCLEAR SUPER POWERS SUCH AS THE UNITED STATES, RUSSIA OR BRITAIN.

South Africa requires moderation and not extremism in these dangerous times, and we have no time for extremism of any sort, whether it comes from the left or from the right. Sir, I love your people, the Afrikaners, and as a child of twelve-years-old I was taught the arts of tanning leather and blacksmithing in the old Dutch tradition by an old Afrikaner, Mr Hennie Swanepoel, and the knowledge I received from that old man enabled me to survive where others would have perished in my long journeys through Africa. It is in his name that I say to you: do not start something that you will not be able to stop.

I beg of you to join hands with others of your nation who are working for peace and reconciliation in South Africa, and I want you to know that you cannot turn the clock of history back, and cannot reconquer the black people just as your forefathers conquered them about a century ago. I say to you, Sir, words that I have said to many other people over the last forty years, that South Africa needs peace and not violence and she needs SALVATION and not CRUCIFIXION.

My words must now draw to an end, and the few that remain are directed towards South Africa herself.

I call upon all politicians and leaders in my country to put South Africa first, and their ambitions second.

I call upon all the leaders of parties and organizations to look at those parties and organizations, and to realize that some of them form a barrier to peace and reconciliation in this land.

I say that the South African Government must, as a prelude to negotiations with black leaders and those wishing to co-operate with it, lay down this condition — that all extra parliamentary organizations and groups should disband. These organizations presently create a state of confrontation within South Africa. A state of confrontation which makes it impossible for people of foresight, people who love peace, and people who fear God, to approach each other and talk to each other, fully and frankly as friends.

I also call for the disbanding of all other organizations, which have been formed to serve certain interests in South Africa, or to articulate certain political viewpoints.

There is no need for confrontation or boycott-politics in South Africa, because only in unity will we ever have strength. South Africans cannot shake each others' hand with daggers up their sleeves; and the reason why I call for the disbanding of these organizations is because those people who do not support these organizations see them as a threat and therefore as sources of fear.

I know that there are thousands and thousands of black people who feel intimidated, blackmailed and frightened by the UDF, especially as a result of certain of it's activists who have committed murder and perpetrated all kinds of crime in the name of this organization.

I know that there are many white people who see Inkatha as a threat, and I know that there are thousands of black people who see the AWB both as a challenge to them as black people and as a source of fear for their future.

I say again, that if the different peoples who make up our country must approach each other and shake hands, they must not do so with daggers hidden under their karosses. No-one can talk peace while the assegai of war is hanging by a spider's thread above his head.

I pray that somehow all South Africa's people will be allowed to peacefully and without intimidation elect men and women who will carry their messages to the negotiating-table for them.

Open Letter to all the Leaders of the Black National States Within the Borders of the Republic of South Africa

Dear Sirs,

I call upon you as the people who are in positions of leadership in the various independent and self-governing national states within our country's borders, and to all of you I say:

The time has come when you must get up and step boldly into the arena of history and be counted among those who strove to save South Africa during the darkest hours of her history.

I call upon the leaders of VENDA, BOPHUTHATSWANA, TRANSKEI, LEBOWA, KWANGWANE, KWANDEBELE, KWA-ZULU and GAZANKULU; and I say to you that the dark and fiery clouds of war and mass death are hanging threateningly in our beloved country's skies and that all of you must come out and prepare to face the coming night with the swords and battle-axes of Truth in your hands because if the fiery deluge of war unleashes its waters upon South Africa, you and your countries too will be engulfed. You cannot escape, you cannot desert the country that gave you the power that is now yours, and you are bound by the chains of history to either stand with South Africa or fall with her, and it is in your deepest interests that South Africa survives the deluges of war and sanctions that are about to fall upon her.

But South Africa cannot survive unless you do your share; you must move and move now to gain and hold the love and respect and loyalty of your people at grassroots-level. Just as South Africa is reforming some of her oldest and most obnoxious laws, so I call upon you to do the same for there are laws in your statute books, which you inherited from South Africa, that you must expunge utterly and urgently. There are attitudes in your people's heads that must be changed and changed now and one of these is the vicious and negative tribal discrimination with which all your countries are cursed.

I am appalled by the untraditional and disrespectful way in which women are being treated in some national states within South Africa; and I want to remind you that women are the key to success in any war against the forces of terrorism, and that furthermore the terrorists are aware of this fact, which is why they love to torture women the most when they are intimidating a community and why they go out of their way to recruit as many women as possible into their ranks.

I call upon you not to make the dreadful mistake that the Government of South Africa made time and again to the eventual detriment of this country, namely the mistake of making enemies out of your most brilliant young people and so driving them to seek shelter in the arms of the communists and terrorists. When a young person is in the service of your Government and doing excellent work to create jobs for the teeming thousands in your state, I urge you to treat that person with justice and respect and not to allow jealous and scheming people to ruin the good work that that person has done. When a man or woman from another tribe comes into your state to create something that will feed your starving people do not allow that person to become the toy of your officials many of whom delight in treating people of other tribes like filth.

Understand, all of you, please, that only by creativity, free and unfettered, shall you prevail over the forces of terrorism and that a well contented and happily employed populace has no ear for the siren-song of the ugly Maiden of Subversion. I call upon you to earn the respect of all your people in all ways that you can and weld them into an impenetrable barrier against terrorism immediately.

Take a leaf out of Doctor Hastings Banda's book and prosper! Above all, get the young people on your side for it is their minds that the terrorists are seeking most in your countries and whoever has the youth on his side shall win the coming wars.

I wish I could tell you more you must urgently do; but I have neither the paper not the time, and in any case it is not really my intention to teach you the ways of leading a nation. May the dark Gods of Africa and all our great Ancestors give you vision. Truly you shall all need it in the coming dark days.

Yours faithfully
Credo Vusamazulu Mutwa

An Open Letter to His Excellency, President PW Botha

Lotlamoreng Dam Traditional
Museums
Mafikeng
Republic of Bophuthatswana
November 1986

President PW Botha
President of the Republic of South Africa
The Houses of the South African Parliament
Cape Town

Dear Sir,

I, Credo Vusamazulu Mutwa, have for well over thirty years tried and failed to promote dialogue, peace and understanding between black and white in South Africa. As far back as 1950, I wrote a letter to Dr DF Malan while he was on holiday at Umndoni Park in Natal, appealing to him to treat our people with mercy and understanding and to do his utmost to restrain hotheads in his party from doing things to the black people that might result in bloodshed in South Africa in the future. But my appeal then, as well as others that followed, fell on deaf ears.

I again appealed to Doctor Hendrik Verwoerd when I met him at his farm near the Vaal River, and I also appealed in 1976, by taperecorder, to Mr BJ Vorster your predecessor, also in vain. Now I am appealing to you, Your Excellency, in the sunset hours of my country's history, and I am appealing to you in front of the whole world, PLEASE DO NOT ALLOW MY COUNTRY AND YOURS TO PERISH IN THE FLAMES OF A RACE WAR. YOU HAVE THE POWER TO GRANT MY CHILDREN AND YOURS A PEACEFUL FUTURE, A FREE AND JUST SOUTH AFRICA,

AND I AM CALLING UPON YOU TO USE THAT POWER OR ELSE EARN YOURSELF THE CONTEMPT OF ALL FUTURE SOUTH AFRICANS.

I say that there is no need whatsoever for violence and bloodshed to escalate in our country, and I say that even now you can, like Our Lord Jesus Christ, cry "halt" to the tempest and cry "be still" to the angry waves. I beg of you not to fall into the trap into which your predecessors fell time and time again, the trap of seeing the problems facing South Africa as being of a purely political nature, because our country's problems are HUMAN and will be solved by HUMAN means and not by political means.

There is too much fear, hatred, suspicion and distrust in South Africa and these HUMAN things cannot be eradicated by empty political speeches or by dramatic flourishes and curlicues of a politician's pen. The truth must be sought out, identified and faced squarely and then dealt with speedily and accordingly.

Sir, you and your Government must face the brutal truth that tens of thousands of our people live in a bloody, crime-ridden environment in black townships. Some of the black leaders you bade us elect, the so-called Urban Councillors are corrupt, bribe-taking villains, who should not be allowed to hold such important offices again in the future.

I call your attention to the sordid spectacle of what is happening in Soweto at this moment, and ask you whether what is happening in Soweto is in South Africa's interests or not — especially in these days when conflict shows every sign of escalating in our country.

I call on you to abolish the councils EVERYWHERE in South Africa and replace them with groups of people who would have the interests of their people at heart, and who would take an oath in public to run clean administrations in the black townships.

I call upon you, Sir, to outlaw RACISM in all its forms in South Africa immediately, and I appeal to the entire western world not to turn its back upon you in your efforts to reform this land, because if it does so then we shall all truly perish.

But I urge you, Sir, to act with all speed, for the Bird of History has taken off and we appear to have lost all control over its flight.

Yours faithfully,
Credo Vusamazulu Mutwa

Afterword

Once more I pray to God almighty, although my soul is strangely uneasy, that may He or She, the All-Highest, grant us peace, even though the dark shadows of conflict, death and pain, are gathering in the red skies of our country.

Although my words may be the bleatings of an old goat lost upon the rocky mountainside, let God and the gods hear me as I plead once more:

LET NOT MY COUNTRY DIE!

Maps

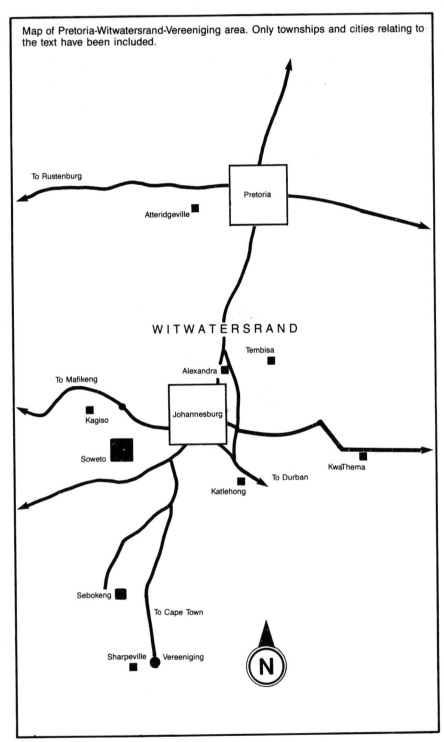

Map of Pretoria-Witwatersrand-Vereeniging area. Only townships and cities relating to the text have been included.

SOWETO

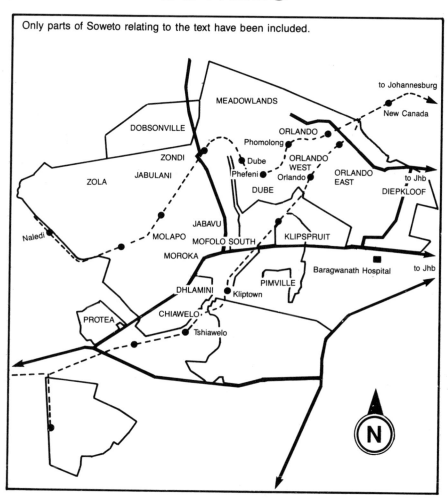

Only parts of Soweto relating to the text have been included.

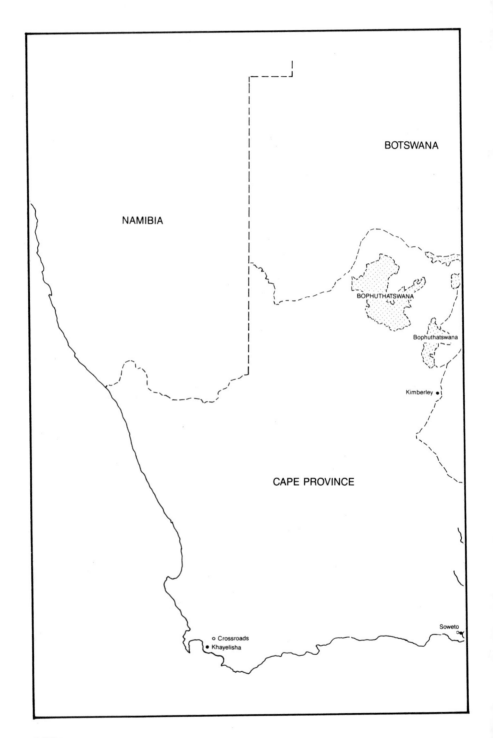

BOTSWANA

NAMIBIA

BOPHUTHATSWANA

Bophuthatswana

Kimberley ●

CAPE PROVINCE

Soweto

○ Crossroads
● Khayelisha

200

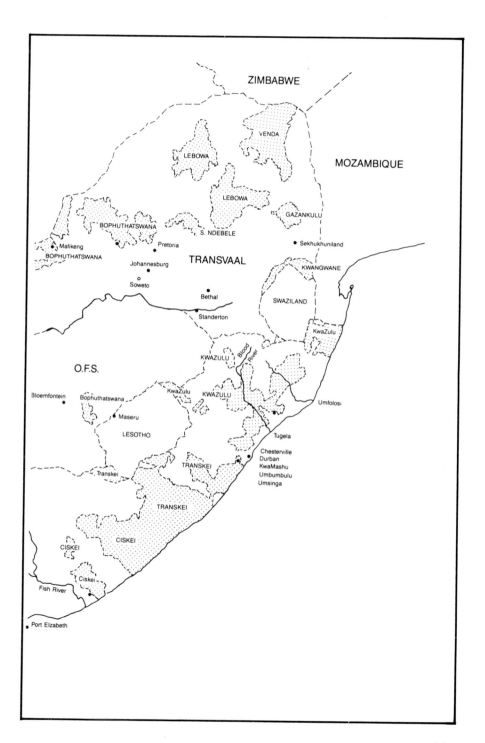

ZIMBABWE

VENDA

MOZAMBIQUE

LEBOWA

LEBOWA

GAZANKULU

BOPHUTHATSWANA

S. NDEBELE

Mafikeng

BOPHUTHATSWANA

Pretoria

Sekhukhuniland

KWANGWANE

Johannesburg

TRANSVAAL

Soweto

Bethal

SWAZILAND

Standerton

KwaZulu

KWAZULU

Blood River

O.F.S.

Bloemfontein

Bophuthatswana

KwaZulu

KWAZULU

KWAZULU

Maseru

Umfolosi

LESOTHO

Tugela

Chesterville

TRANSKEI

Durban

Transkei

KwaMashu

Umbumbulu

Umsinga

TRANSKEI

CISKEI

CISKEI

Ciskei

Fish River

Port Elzabeth

201

Notes

Notes

1 **Eichmann, (Karl) Adolf** (1906-1962). Austrian-born Eichmann was head of the German Gestapo's Jewish Extermination Department in World War II. He was sentenced to death on December 15, 1961 by an Israeli court for crimes against the Jewish people and against humanity.

2 **Kurt Waldheim** (1918-) is the President of Austria and was the former head of the United Nations. It has been alleged that he witnessed Nazi atrocities during the Second World War.

3 **Herrenvolk** is a word that means superior or chosen race; and it was used during The Third Reich to unite German people.

4 **Feldhure** was the word used for women selected for sex for Nazi soldiers and guards in concentration camps.

5 **My-Lai** (also May Lai). Two hundred unarmed civilians were murdered in the South Vietnam village of My-Lai. The massacre was carried out by American soldiers on March 16, 1968, and many were found guilty.

6 **Azanian People's Organization (AZAPO).** AZAPO started in 1978 to politicize and mobilize black workers, through the philosophy of black consciousness, to strive for legitimate rights. It also works towards establishing an education system for the needs of Azania and to expose the exploitive system and devise basic human rights. It also encourages an equal distribution of land.

7 **United Democratic Front (UDF).** The UDF was founded in 1983. It consists of a number of provincial bodies seeking to unite different civic and youth associations and trade unions opposed to apartheid. The UDF claims to have two million members, and more than 600 affiliated organizations.

8 **Inkatha.** Revived and given new meaning by Chief Mangosuthu Buthelezi, Inkatha is ostensibly a Zulu cultural organization that has its roots in the early 1920s.

9 **Afrikaner Weerstandsbeweging.** The AWB is an ultra right-wing organization that believes there is only one white nation in Africa — the Afrikaner. The AWB uses a symbol that resembles the Nazi Swastika. It has a militant wing called the Brandwag.

10 **al-Qaddafi, Muammar** (1942-). Muammar al-Qaddafi (also Gaddafi) was a Libyan soldier and a politician. A Bedouin, he led the coup that deposed King Idris I in

1969. As chairman of the Revolutionary Command Council, he became Prime Minister of Libya 1970-72, and President from 1972. He directs a puritan Islamic and socialist regime close to the USSR and hostile to the Egyptian-Israeli detente and to the USA.

11 **Miwok Reservation.** It is a reservation in Northern California where the last remaining members of the Miwok North American Indian tribe are now living.

12 **Sweat Lodge.** A ritual "sauna-bath" of the Red Indians.

13 **Paiute.** The Paiute are two distinct American Indian groups speaking the language of the Numic group of the Uto-Aztecan family. They now number a few thousand people who live on reservations in the USA. They fought against the appropriation of their land by whites until 1874 when the last land was taken.

14 **Tualumne.** An Indian valley in Northern California.

15 The **Influx Control Laws** were laid to control the flow of black labour into the white areas, particularly the towns and cities. They consist of the laws allocating labour between sectors and regions.

16 The **FBI** is the largest investigation agency in the US Federal Government. It is responsible for investigating where federal interest is concerned. The FBI is part of the US Department of Justice.

17 The **CIA** is the principal intelligence agency and counter intelligence agency of the US Government. It was created in 1947.

18 *Nineteen Eight-Four.* This was a book written by George Orwell and published in 1949. It is a vision of a totalitarian world whose rulers exploit psychological and technical discoveries to retain and consolidate power.

19 **Tyler, Wat (or Walter)** (died 1381). He was an English rebel and leader who led the Kentishmen (men from Essex) in the peasants' revolt (1381).

20 **Malan, Daniel Francois** (1874-1959). Malan was a South African Nationalist Politician. Born in the Cape Colony (now Cape Province), he was a preacher and journalist before entering politics. In 1936 he became leader of the opposition and was Prime Minister from 1948-1954.

21 **Verwoerd, Hendrik Frensch** (1901-1966). A South African politician, he became Prime Minister in 1958. Assassinated in 1966.

22 **Grey, Sir George Edward** (1812-1898). He was English colonial administrator and became governor of South Australia (1841) and then New Zealand (1845-53). There he ended the war with the Maoris, to whom he was sympathetic. He was Governor of the Cape Colony from 1954-61. He returned to New Zealand and was appointed Liberal Prime Minister (1877-1879).

23 **Nationalist Government of 1948.** The National Party came to power in South Africa in 1948, with Dr DF Malan as the new Prime Minister. The new government was determined to make South Africa an independent republic, and to carry on the apartheid system already established.

24 **Dube, John Langalibalele.** John Dube was born of royal blood of the Ngcobo tribe. He was educated at the Amanzimtoti Institute (new Adams College) and Oberlin College, Ohio USA. After returning to Natal in 1895 as a teacher, he founded the Ohlanga Mission School (high school) see note 27. Later he became first chairman of the South African Native National Congress of which he was a founder memeber and the first black man to receive a degree from a South African University.

25 **Washington, Booker T** (1856-1915). An American negro educationist and author of *Up From Slavery* , Washington became principle of Tuskegee Institute in Alabama.

26 **Kitchener, Herbert Horatio** (1850-1916). lst Earl and British soldier. While still a cadet at the Royal Military Academy, he served with the French army in the Franco-Prussian War. He was appointed Chief of Staff in the Boer War (1900).

27 **Ohlange Mission College.** Now a secondary school in Natal see note 24.

28 **African National Congress (ANC)**. The ANC was originally known as the South African Native National Congress, which was formed in Bloemfontein in 1912. The name was changed to the ANC in 1923. It grew to become the principal organization campaigning for black political rights and was banned by the government along with the PAC on April 8, 1960. Nelson Mandela had controlled the ANC up to his imprisonment and is still regarded as its leader.

29 **The Land Act of 1936**. (known as the Native Trust and Land Act of 1936). Land totalling 17.6 million morgen in all four provinces was set aside for black people. The acts, also known as the native acts, effectively derprived the blacks of any right to buy or own land outside the reserves.

30 **Alexander** (known as the Great) (356-323BC). King of Macedon (from 337), he first distinguished himself at the battle of Chaeronea (338) against the Thebans, while his father was still king. He was only 19 when his father was murdered and he succeeded to the throne. Alexander won his first victory on the River Granicus, and in 333 marched through Phrygia to Issus, where he defeated King Darius III and captured his family and treasures. He then conquered Syria and Phoenicia and, rejecting offers of peace, reached Eygpt where the inhabitants, tired of the harsh Persian rule, welcomed him. In the following year he founded Alexandria. He was hailed as divine by many of his followers and had shown signs of megalomania. With an army that probably never exceeded 35,000 fighting men, he came to rule an empire stretching from Italy to India.

31 **Darius III** (died 330BC). King of Persia from 336. His reign was marked by the conquest of his empire by Alexander the Great.

32 **Rondavel**. Round hut with a thatched roof.

33 **Inyangas** are black traditional healers and herbalists. There are a number of classes of inyangas, which are either traditional healers, herbalists or both. See notes 40-42.

34 **Sangomas** are (mostly) female diviners and clairvoyants, whose primary function it is to heal.

35 **Divining Bones and powers**. Instuments used by the sanusis and the sangomas with which to learn about future events and diagnose illness.

36 **Coming out Dances**. Initiation dances for new sangomas and inyangas.

37 **Verkrampte**. Over Conservative.

38 **Adrian Boshier** (1939-1978) was the subject of Lyall Watson's book, *Lightning Bird*. He was deeply interested in African life, and an adventurer who ventured into some of the least accessible parts of southern Africa, where he lived for many years. He revived some of the ancient mysteries of Africa and discovered prehistoric artifacts, ancient cave paintings and rituals of African witchcraft.

39 **Dr Lyall Watson** was born in Africa and is a scientist and writer — especially of the paranormal. His books include *Supernature* and *Lightning bird*. He has been involved in anthropology, archaeological excavations, palaeontology, biology, botany and medical research.

40 **Moroga class**. A class of traditional healer, whose powers are used to protect villages and people against lightning.

41 **Sanusi**. The highest class of healers. They are regarded as priests by millions of black people. The sanusis know all the ancient secrets of protection and healing. They also serve their communities with psychological and psychiatrical help. The highest of the sanusis is known as the High Sanusi or High Witchdoctor. See note 33.

42 **Mundawa or Lion class**. Also a healer but of a class just below the sanusi.

43 **Dunn, John** was a white trader from Natal who, after travelling to Zululand, acquired guns for Cetshwayo. He sided with Chief Mbulazi in the Zulu civil wars and fought at the battle of Ndondakusuka. He also became a Zulu chief (1856).

44 **Isaacs, Nathaniel** (1808-1872). Isaacs journeyed to the kraal of Shaka and joined

Shaka in battle against the Mbeje. He was a Zulu chief. He arrived in South Africa as a trader from England with the 1820 settlers, and left the Cape in 1833.

45 **Lieutenant Henry Ogle** (1800-1860) was a Natal trader and one of the 1820 (British) settlers. He was a signatory of Shaka's deed of cession (1824) which granted territory around Port Natal to Lieuetenant FG Farewell. Because of the cruelty of Shaka and Dingane, many of their subjects fled to Port Natal and attached themselves to Ogle, who they regarded as their chief. He married an English woman, but fathered many coloured children.

46 **Colenso, Bishop J W.** (1814-1883) Colenso was Bishop of Natal. He translated parts of the new and old testament into Zulu and was called Sobantu (father of the people) by the Zulus. In 1861 he wrote a Zulu-English dictionary. In 1879 he sided with the Zulu king Cetshwayo and campaigned for peace, believing that the British were planning to destroy the Zulu nation.

47 **Stevenson, Robert** (1772-1850). Stevenson was a Scottish engineer and builder of lighthouses who invented intermittent and flashing lights.

48 **Brunel, Sir Isambard Kingdom** (1805-1959). A British engineer, his plans for the Clifton suspension bridge over the River Avon at Bristol, England were adopted in 1831. From 1833 to 1846 he was chief engineer of the Great Western Railway in England. In 1837 he designed the first trans-Atlantic steamer.

49 **Lister, Joseph, 1st Baron** (1827-1912). An English surgeon, born in Essex, he was a great teacher and surgeon. He designed special operating tables and surgical tools, and introduced the use of white operating costumes, emphasizing antiseptic (killing germs) measures.

50 **Nobel, Alfred Bernhard** (1833-1896). A Swedish chemist, Nobel's main interest lay in the development of explosives. He invented dynamite in 1867. From his vast fortunes made from the manufacture of explosives, he established five prizes to be awarded annually for literature, medicine, physics, chemistry and the promotion of peace.

51 **Diesel, Rudolf** (1858-1913). German inventor, born in Paris and moved to England where he studied engineering and thermodynamics in Germany. The engine which bears his name, an internal-combustion engine with fuel ignited by heat following compression, was patented in 1892.

52 **Benz, Karl** (1844 - 1929). German motor car pioneer, he produced (1885) a three-wheeled, chain-driven vehicle with a water-cooled internal-combustion engine using coal gas as fuel. It travelled at a maximum speed of 15 mph.

53 **Marx, Karl Heinrich** (1818-1883). German founder of modern international communism: In conjunction with his friend Friedrich Engels, he wrote the *Communist Manifesto of 1848* for the communist league, of which he was the leader. He also wrote *Das Kapital,* a deep analysis of the economic laws that govern modern society. He ranks as one of the most original and influential thinkers of modern times.

54 **Kingsley, Charles** (1819-1875). English clergyman and author, and one of the founders of the Christian Socialist Movement.

55 **Lawrence, Thomas Edward** (1888-1935). Known as Lawrence of Arabia, he wrote *Seven Pillars of Wisdom.* He led the Arabs against the Turks in the war of 1914-1918. And was known for his anti-Semitism and his remarks towards dark skinned people.

56 **Smith, Joseph** (1805-1844) An American religious teacher, he founded the Mormon Church. He was arrested on charges of conspiracy and murdered by a mob in prison.

57 **Moffat, Robert.** (ca 1800). Robert Moffat was a well known missionary in South Africa in the early 1800s. He was known for his work with the Tswana and worked with his son-in-law David Livingstone at building a mission station at Kuruman in the Cape Province. See note 58.

58 **Livingstone, David** (1813-1873). Scottish missionary and explorer.

59 **George Stechmannn.** A Christian missionary. At the time of publishing, very little information could be found on Stechmann.

60 **Dingane** (died 1840, his birth date is not known). Dingane was the Zulu king who assinated his half-brother Shaka to become king of the Zulus. The Voortrekker leader Piet Retief tried to negotiate with Dingane in 1837 for a large tract of land, but Retief and his men were were executed on the signing of the treaty on orders from Dingane. See note 82.

61 **Owen, Rev. Francis** (1802-1854). Owen arrived at the Cape in March 1837. He travelled to Zululand and with the consent of Dingane, he established a mission at Dingane's kraal.

62 **Montezuma II** (or Moctezuma) (1466-1520) was the last of the Aztec emperors of Mexico (1503-20).

63 **Cortez, Hernando** (1485-1547) was a Spanish explorer and administrator. In 1518 he led an army of 508 men to explore Mexico.

64 **Mosaic Code** or Mosaic Law is the ancient Hebrew law contained in the first five books of the old testament.

65 **Bishop James Hannington** was an English Anglican missionary and first bishop of Eastern Equatorial Africa (June 1884). He was killed in 1885 by the King Mwanga of Buganda.

66 **King Mwanga.** Last King of the Kingdom of Buganda, now Uganda.

67 **Kruger, (Stephanus Johannes) Paulus** (1825-1904). Boer Politician. The northward Great Trek took him as a child to the Transvaal, the new territory outside the sphere of British rule. He took part in the early phase of the Boer War and in 1900 sailed to Europe in the hope of obtaining support for the Boers. He did not return to Africa and died in Switzerland.

68 **The Anglo Boer War** (1899-1902) was the war in which the Boers defended the republics of the Transvaal and Free State against Great Britain. Alfred Milner, the Cape High Commissioner, saw the two republics — especially the Transvaal and its goldfields — as a threat to British supremacy in South Africa.

69 **Griquas** are people of mixed descent, the name Griqua was adopted name in 1813.

70 The **Kimberley Diamond Fields** were the claims staked by people after diamonds were discovered in the region. The fields were opened in 1871 with hundreds of people staking claims. The claims eventually led to the development of the Big Hole, the largest man-made whole in the world.

71 **Advocate Okert J Bekker** was a leading newspaper man and prominent advocate.

72 **Bitter-Einder** is the Afrikaans term for a die-hard or to the very last man attitude — to the bitter end.

73 **General Christiaan Rudolph De Wet** (1854-1922). A Boer soldier and politician, he was a successful guerrilla leader in the Boer War and never accepted the political implications of defeat. He believed that the outbreak of the First World War provided an opportunity to re-establish a Boer republic and he led a rising against the Loius Botha government.

74 **Rooinekke.** A derogatory name for the British. It means rednecks and it was used by the Boers.

75 **Putu.** A porridge made from maize meal, includes sour milk.

76 **Broederbond.** A secret cultural organization founded in May 1918 with the object of secretly furthering the interests of the Afrikaner people.

77 **Ossewa-Brandwag (OB).** Started as a cultural movement, the OB gradually became very influential in the political arena. The OB supported Hitler's political philosophy.

78 **1914 Rebellion.** The rebellion arose over the Union of South Africa's declaration to enter the First World War. Many Afrikaners opposed fighting with the British against Germany. Under the command of General K de la Rey, the Afrikaners in-

tended to launch a protest against the British attack on South West Africa.

79 **1922 General Strike.** Due to the 1920-23 depression, miners in South Africa announced wage cuts and 20 000 white miners went on strike, meaning 180 000 blacks had no work either. The strikers decided to use force to overthrow the Smuts government. The situation deteriorated and martial law was declared.

80 **Laager.** Defensive encampment inside a circle of ox wagons.

81 **The Great Trek.** Emigration of thousands of Afrikaans speaking frontier farmers from the British Cape Colony to the Transvaal. It was an exodus of Afrikaners from British colonialism and oppression.

82 **Murder of Piet Retief.** The famous Voortrekker leader of the Great Trek was killed by Dingane on February 6, 1838. See note 60-61.

83 **Battle of Blood River.** After Dingane had Piet Retief killed, Andries Pretorius avenged his fellow voortrekker's death. On December 16, 1838 he fought a battle against the Zulus on the Buffalo River (later to be known as Blood River).

84 **Voortrekker Monument.** The monument in Pretoria was officially opened in 1948. It was built in remembrance of the Voortrekkers who trekked from the Cape to the Transvaal.

85 **Wit mens** means **gentleman** and is used as a racist insult.

86 **Sjambok.** A leather or plastic whip.

87 **Dondered.** To be beaten up or thrashed.

88 **Pass Offences.** One of the major pass offences was when blacks tried to live and work illegally in the towns. The sentence was imprisonment.

89 **Locations.** In 1846 a commission recommended that a number of locations (or reserves) be established for the black people. In the 1860s municipal locations were built to provide accommodation for the black people flowing into the towns.

90 **Knobkierie.** A Walking stick also used as a weapon, a knobkieri is usually carved of wood and contains a thick knob at one end.

91 **Kwela-Kwela.** Means "hurry-up, hurry-up" or "climb in, climb in." A name given to the huge police trucks into which blacks were herded for pass offence arrests.

92 **Peri-Urban Board.** The board for the development of areas for blacks around the urban white areas.

93 **Strijdom, Johannes Gerhardus** (1893-1958). South African Politician. He entered South African parliament in 1929 and became Prime Minister (1954-58).

94 **Bantu Education.** Education system for black children brought in by Dr HF Verwoerd. In 1955 the Government submitted a legislation to apply apartheid at a cultural level, because it was felt it was 'wrong to force a white man's culture onto the black man.' It was decided there should be two types of education, white education and black education.

95 **Barotse.** Large tribe in south west Zambia

96 **Separate Development.** A policy adopted by the South African government to allow blacks to develop on their own in the "homelands." It is a major policy under the system of apartheid.

97 **Pass Laws and Dom-pas.** See also note 15. Slang name for identity documents or pass. Direct translation from Afrikaans is "stupid pass."

98 **Bantu Affairs.** The Bantu Affairs Administration Board — sevicing the interest of the black population in the townships — was unpopular, and in 1976, after the Soweto Riots, it was announced by the Government that community councils would replace the Urban Bantu Councils in the townships and assume certain functions of the Bantu Affairs Administration Board.

99 **Koornhof, Dr Piet.** (1925 -) He was Deputy minister of Bantu Administration in 1968, and Deputy minister of Bantu Education and Bantu Affairs in 1970. From 1978 to 1984 he held the post of Minister of Cooperation and Development and said

there would be no more forced removals of blacks from townships.

100 **Shaka.** Zulu king (ca 1787-1828). After the death of King Dingiswayo, Shaka rose to sieze the Zulu kingdom under his father, Senzagakhona. He then transformed the Zulu army into the most powerful fighting force in south east Africa. He was assinated by his half-brother Dingane.

101 **Moshoeshoe** King (also Moshweshwe or Mushweshwe) (ca 1786- 1870). Moshshoeshoe was the founder and first paramount chief of the Basotho. He established his kingdom on the top of a flat-topped mountain, which was named Thaba Bosiu.

102 **Indunas.** Leaders in tribal government.

103 **van Riebeck, Jan** (1619-1670). He was sent by the Dutch East India Company (1652) to found a settlement at the Cape of Good Hope. He remained for ten years, the settlement forming the nucleus of the South African Republic of today.

104 **Hottentots.** Short stocky people who lived in the Cape of Good Hope area in the 17th and 18th centuries. They were encountered by the settlers and became a major feature in the history of the settlements. They were used as slaves and servants and revolted against forced labour.

105 **Koppie.** A small Hill (Afrikaans).

106 **Kraal.** A village of huts enclosed by a fence.

107 **Cillie Commission of Inquiry.** As a result of Soweto Riots, Government appointed a commission of enquiry. Mr Justice PM Cillie was appointed by the House of Assembly as the only member of the commission.

108 **Marquis de Sade** (1740-1814). A French author, he was imprisoned many times for crimes of wanton cruelty (hence the word sadism). To avoid a death penalty, he went to live in Italy. He published a number of novels which are in part sexual fantasy and in part psuedo-philosophical attempts to justify his vices.

109 **Department of Bantu Education.** The department overseeing black education, which is very often at the centre of controversy surrounding the education of blacks in South Africa.

110 **Bantu Administration Board.** This body is represented by boards in the major centres that supplied pass books and controlled the influx of blacks into white areas.

111 **Urban Bantu Council.** Community councils (for example the Soweto City Counci) replaced the Urban Bantu Councils after the 1976 Soweto Riots.

112, 113 **Thirty year and Ninety-nine year Leasehold Schemes.** In 1972 the Bantu Affairs Department promised more blacks would be allowed to bring their wives into the urban areas, if there was housing. In 1975, the Bantu Affairs reintroduced the thirty year leaseholds, but said that only blacks who became citizens of their homelands would receive privileges in white areas. After the 1976 riots, the citizenship proviso was dropped from the leasehold scheme, and it was said that blacks could buy their homes for all time, and could sell or bequeath them to their children. In 1978 the Bantu Act was ammended allowing a ninety-nine year leasehold, but the ammendment appeared to disqualify children, born after the independence of homelands, from inhereting such rights, because they were foreigners. Property rights were granted on ninety-nine year leaseholds and in 1983 it was stated that the leaseholds would continue in perpetuity.

114 **Traditional Museum Village.** Built by Credo Mutwa in the centre of Soweto. The objective of the exercise was to bring the black man closer to his roots and culture.

115 **Steve Biko.** (Died in detention in September 1977). Biko was a key figure in the black consciousness movement. He died while in the custody of the security police in Pretoria and the exact events leading up to his death are unknown.

116 **Tri-Cameral Parliament.** Tri-Cam came about under the new constitution of September 1984: the House of Assembly with white members, The House of Representatives, representing the coloureds, and the House of Delegates, representing the

Indians. The President initiates legislation and resolves disputes between the houses.

117 **Suppression of Communism Act.** It Became a law on June 26, 1950, banning the South African Communist Party from promoting the aims of communism.

118 **Terrorism Act.** The act provides that a suspected terrorist can be detained for an indefinite period without trial, and if circumstances warrant it, the detainee can be visited once a fortnight by a magistrate. No information regarding the detainee is made public.

119 **Mandela, Nelson.** (1918-). Mandela joined the African national Congress (ANC) in 1944 and was one of the founder memebers of the Youth League of which he was made president in 1950. In July 1963 police closed in on a Rivonia farmhouse headquarters of *Umkonto we Sizwe*, the military wing of the ANC, and found Mandela's diary and document in his writing *How to Be a Good Communist*. During the Rivonia trial Mandela was sentenced to life imprisonment.

120 **Sisulu, Walter.** (1912-). Sisulu joined the ANC in 1940 and was one of the first members who steered the ANC into a more militant and active role. He was arrested on October 1963 during the raid on the headquaters of *Umkonto We Sizwe* on a charge of sabotage. He was sentenced to life imprisonment for planning acts of sabotage.

121 **Baluba vs Luluwa Wars.** Violent tribal wars between the two tribes in the then Belgian Congo.

122 **Biafran War,** May 30 1967. **Col Odumegwu Ojukwu** excised the coastal part of Nigeria from the Federal Government of Nigeria, under Gen. Yakubu Gowon. Gowon refused to recognize Biafra and the country was cut off from the coast resulting in the mass-starvation of several million people.

123 **Col Ojukwu.** See biafran war.

124 **Bahutus.** Ruwanda tribe of tall black people. They often went to war with the Watutsi tribe.

125 **Watutsi.** see note 124.

126 **Ruwanda-Urundi** (Rwanda). Formerly Ruanda-Burundi and part of German East Africa (now Tanganyika).

127 **Buthelezi, Chief Mangosuthu,** Buthelezi is the President of Inkatha and the chief minister of KwaZulu. He has repeateldy refused to accept the homeland status of independence, similar to Bophuthatswana.

128 **Shivhakava Tree.** The sacred tree in Zulu tradition which is believed to be the Tree of life referred to in Zulu tradition.

129 **Musutaraya Monster.** A mythical sphinx like monster that appears in Zulu legend.

130 **Edelstein, Melville.** Edelstein was killed on June 16, 1976 (Soweto Riots) by enraged Soweto students. A welfare officer, he did years of service in Soweto and he undertook a study of the attitudes of Soweto matriculants, published in 1972. He found that influx control was regarded as the student's greatest grievrance second to inadequate political rights.

131 **Dlamini Clan.** The Swazi royal family.

132 **Mukaranga.** A member of the Karanga tribe of Zimbabwe

133 **Justice Joseph Francis Ludorf** (1913-1982). Justice Ludorf was a supreme court judge for 23 years and retired in 1973.

134 *Indaba My Children.* The first book written by Credo Mutwa in which he reveals much about African life and culture.

135 **Central African Federation.** (The Nyasaland Protectorate.) A political unit created in 1953 that embraced the British Southern Rhodesia, Northern Rhodesia and Nyasaland. It was under the control of the British Colonial Office in London.

136 **Southern Rhodesian.** The country achieved independence from Britain in 1964 (Unilateral Declaration of Independence — UDI in 1965) as Rhodesia. After a long bush war, majority rule was declared in 1980 under new prime minister Robert

Mugabe.

137 **Nothern Rhodesian.** Northern Rhodesia achieved independence in 1964 to become Zambia.

138 **Nyasaland.** (Now Malawi). Nyasaland became self-governing in 1964.

139 **Joshua Nkomo.** The Marxist leader of the Patriotic Front in Rhodesia who fought the Rhodesians in the long bush war that led to the independance of Zimbabwe.

140 **Kaunda, (David) Kenneth** (1924-). The first President of Zambia. He entered politics in Northern Rhodesia (now Zambia) in 1948. He founded the Zambia African National Congress in 1958, which was reformed in 1961 after being banned.

141 **Banda, Dr Hastings Kamazu** (1906 -). The life president of Malawi, he was educated at a mission school. He emigrated to the USA where, after fifteen years work, his savings allowed him to take degrees in philosophy and medicine. He left the USA, and went to England where he practiced until 1953. From 1958 he led the independence movement in Nyasaland and headed the Malwai Congress Party founded in 1959. When the country attained self-government in 1963 Banda became prime minister, an office he retained until July 1964 when Malawi became independent.

142 **Welensky, Sir Roy** (1907 -). He became Rhodesian prime minister in 1956 and played an extensive role in the Cental African Federation.

143 **State of Emergency.** Anti-apartheid rioting led to the imposition of a state of emergency in certain areas on 20 July 1985, and was lifted on 7 March 1986, it was again imposed on June 12, 1986 to quell futher rioting. The first state of emergency to be imposed in South Africa was declared on March 30, 1960 as a result of massive rioting against the pass laws. It was terminated on August 31, 1960.

144 **Smith, Ian Douglas** (1919 -). Smith became Rhodesian prime minister in 1964 and the following year he declared UDI, fearing that Britain would hasten majority rule in the country. He stepped down to Robert Mugabe in 1980. See note 136.

145 **Black Power** was a movement of American Negroes during the last decade to secure a rightful place in American society.

146 **Negritude.** A literary and philosophical movement asserting black identity and cultural values.

147 **Black Consciousness.** The main objective of black consiousness is to overcome the "dependence complex" many blacks have in relation to the whites, and to assert the black man's self reliance to give him a sense of worth in society.

148 **Nyerere, Julius Kambarage** (1921-). Tanzanian politician. In 1954 he founded the Tanganyika African National Union with a policy aimed at independence. In his successful pursuit of this aim he was successively appointed Chief Minister of Tanganyika in 1960 and Prime Minister when independence was granted in 1961. He later became President in 1962 when a republic was proclaimed. When Zanzibar, after its revolution in 1964, became linked with Tanganyika, he became president of the combined country known thereafter as Tanzania.

149 **Idi Amin.** (1925-) In 1971 the imfamous tyrant's army overthrew President Milton Obote and Amin became president. In 1979 he fled the country following the invasion of Uganda by Ugandan exiles, which were backed by the Tanzanian government.

150 **Freedom Charter (ANC).** A socialist democracy with equal rights for all races was demanded and adopted at a "Congress of the People" in 1955. Although it was free of communist terminology and concepts, it propogated radical and revolutionary change in South Africa.

151 **King Zulu.** He was the first king of the Zulus.

152 **Robert Sobukwe.** (1924-1978). After extensive studying Robert Sobukwe became a teacher and in 1948 joined the Youth League of the ANC. His ideas were "Government of the Africans, by the Africans, for the Africans" and in 1958 he campaigned

to breakaway from the ANC to form the Pan Africanist Congress (PAC). He was elected president of the PAC soon after its formation. After studying law he opened a practice in 1975.

153 **Comrades**. A general term used for youths fighting the plight of blacks and helping in the "black struggle." Althought it is applied in the communistic sense it has tribal and linguistic implications.

154 **Kaizer Chiefs**. A popular South African soccer team.

155 **Khrushchev, Nikita Sergeyevich** (1894-1971). Russian politician, born in Kalinkova, Kursk Province. He joined the Communist Party in 1918 and began his career as party organiser at the age of 35. He was elected to the Politburo in 1939 and was Secretary of the Moscow Province Communist Party from 1949-1953. He was forced out of office in October 1964 and passed into obscure retirement.

156 **Stalin, Joseph** (1879-1953). For nearly 30 years he was the leader of the Russian people. Originally he studied for a priesthood, but became and active revolutionary and took part in the civil war after 1917. After Lenin's death, he ousted Trotsky and became the outstanding figure. He modernised agriculture on socialist lines by ruthless means, and his series of five year plans, from 1929, made Russia an industrial power. On the German invasion in 1941, he assumed military leadership, and later attended allied war conferences.

157 **Mobuto Sese Seko**. Statesman and president of Zaire. He succeeded to power in 1965 with a coup, and changed the name of the country from the Democratic Republic of the Congo to the Republic of Zaire.

158 **Mao Ze-Dong (also Mao Tse-Tung)** (1893-1976). Chinese Communist Leader. He was one of the 12 founder members of the Chinese Communist Party in Shanghai in 1921, and set up more than 50 trade unions between 1925 and 1927. He proclaimed the foundation of the Chinese Peoples' Republic in 1949 and served as Chairman from 1949 to 1959.

159 **Ntsu Mokhehle**. He is the leader of the Basotholand People's Party and was Leabua Johnathan's chief political adversary.

160 **Leabua Johathan** was Prime Minister of Lesotho. In 1976 he met with BJ Vorster in Cape Town and agreed that a peaceful co-existence and vigilance against communism were in their common interest. His government was overthrown in January 1986. Lesotho is now ruled by a Military Council led by Maj Gen Justin Kekhanya.

161 See note 101

162 **Mugabe, Robert Gabriel** (1925-) First Prime Minister of independent Zimbabwe (1980). After training he went to Northern Rhodesia (now Zambia) to teach and from there to Ghana in 1958. Later he became secretary-general of the Zimbabwe African National Union (ZANU).

163 **Vorster, Balthazar Johannes** (known as John) (1915-1983). South African Prime Minister (1966-1978) and elected President in 1978.

164 **Natal Midlands Administration Board**. This board is to be abolished at the end of 1986, it deals with the townships of Natal, and is soley for black projects.

165 **Vladimir Lenin** (1870-1924). Russian revolutionary leader and statesman. From 1893 to 1917 he worked underground in Russia and abroad for the revolutionary cause. During this time the Social democratic party was formed. Lenin was the leader of the Bolsheviks. In 1922 his new economic policy somewhat modified the intensive drive towards planned industrial development.

166 **Bolshevik**. Member of the Revolutionary Party led by Lenin which seized power in Russia in 1917.

167 **Chernobyl**. Russian nuclear disaster where the Chernobyl power station reactor was destroyed. The fuel disintigrated, the reactor head blew off because of a generation of steam, and there was a chemical explosion, which caused high levels of radiation

in the area, and radioactive clouds travelled as far as England.

168 **Robert Pavlita.** Czechoslovakian scientist experimenting with the power of the human mind.

169 **Baganda Blacksmiths** of Uganda make spears and weapons for war and ceremonial purposes.

170 **Kavirondo Blacksmiths.** Also of Uganda, the Kavirondo balcksmiths also make weapons.

171 **Wagogo** blacksmiths of East Africa are believed to be the earlist iron-age smelters in the world.

172 **Manyandisa Shatti** is a sun-worshipping ceremony.

173 **Saladin** (Salah-al Din Yusuf Ibn Ayyub) (1137-1193) Sultan of Egypt and Syria (from 1174). Born in Mesopotamia of Kurdish origin, he succeeded his uncle as vizier of Egypt (1169). His chivalry was much admired by the Crusaders and he was a just and efficient ruler as well as a fine soldier.

174 The **Mayan** (Maya singular) were American Indian people, remarkable for their art and knowledge of astronomy, who lived from circa 300 in Guatemala (The Old Empire) in city states, and migrated in the 9th century to Yucatan in East Mexico (New Empire) where thier culture partially merged with that of the Toltecs, but disintegrated in mid 15th Century owing to civil wars. It was found in decay by the invading Spaniards in 1511.

175 **Jim Hurtak.** President of the Future Sciences Organization in America, he has visited South Africa on several occasions.

176 **Favelas** The shanty towns of Rio de Janiro where a large part of the population lives. Located on steep hillsides and shorelines

177 **Kupugani.** Began in 1962 as an organization to combat malnutrition and teach people what to eat for good health. Kupugani provided those foods at a low cost to people of low income groups.

178 **Operation Snowball.** The organization began 20 years ago after a snowstorm, an individual sent a donation to help people who were suffering because of the cold. It is presently being run by the Star newspaper, and money is collected annually to buy blankets for needy people of all races.

179 **Operation Hunger.** A national organization that began in 1980 as a response to the need felt by voluntary organizations. Its aims are to relieve hunger and poverty in rural areas. There are two aims, the short term aim of hunger relief, and the long term aim of self help.

180 **Bantu Investment Corporation.** Started in May 1959 to establish black industries in the homelands.

181 **Urban Foundation.** Established by Harry Oppenheimer and Anton Rupert with the aim of improving the quality of life for urban black people.

182, 183, 184 and 185 **Transkei, Ciskei, Venda, Bophuthatswana Homelands.** These areas were to become the national homes of all blacks in South Africa, including those residing in white areas. Verwoerd wanted to base homeland government on the traditional government systems of the blacks. Transkei received territorial authority and self government in 1957 (the first homeland to do so). Chief Kaiser Matanzima drew up constitutions in 1962. From 1972-1974 the following obtained self-government. Bophuthastswana (Lucas Mangope as Chief Minister), Ciskei (Lennox Sebe as Chief Minister), Lebowa (Dr Cedric Phatudi Chief Minister) Gazankulu (Prof. Hudson Ntsaninsi Chief Minister) Venda (Patrick Mpephu Chief Minister) Basotho Qwaqwa (Wessels Mota Chief Minister).

186 **Katangese Succession.** (Congo) A week after independence the Congolese army mutinied and whites fled the country. Moise Tshombe declared indepedence of Katanga while he retained Belguin army officers.

187 **Toivo Ja Toivo, Herman.** A founder member of The South West African People's organization (SWAPO), he was released from prison on March 1, 1984 by the South African Government. No reason was given for his release. He had served 16 years of a 20 year sentence for seeking to overthrow the Namibian Administration installed by South Africa. He was imprisoned on Robben Island.

188 **Pan Africanist Congress.** The PAC was founded in 1959 by a number of "Africanists" who had broken away from the ANC. It was banned with the ANC in 1960 under the Unlawful Organisation Act.

189 **Josias Madzunya.** One of the founder members of the PAC, he was one of the first "Africanists" to promote the motto of the PAC "Africa for the Africans".

190 **Pollsmoor Prison.** State penitentiary which houses many political prisoners, including Nelson Mandela.

191 **Armistice of 1918.** An armistice was signed by the Germans on November 11, 1918, ending the First World War. The Treaty of Versailles was signed with Germany in 1919.

192 **Third Reich.** Germany under the leadership of Adolf Hitler (1933-45)

193 **Chiang Kai-Shek** (1887-1975) Chinese soldier and statesman. Whilst an officer cadet he became involved in the successful revolution (1911) against the last Manchu emperor and was a loyal adherent of Sun Yat-sen, who in 1921 established himself as president of the Republican Government. Chiang Kai-Shek was appointed leader of the nationalists and eliminated the rival Communist Government.

194 **Dalai Lama.** A spiritual leader or priest. Highest lineage of reincarnate lamas, last of whom was sent into exile in 1959 after being temporal ruler of Tibet.

195 **Chutzpah.** Yiddish for "cheek."

196 **Glen Eagles Agreement.** An agreement signed by a number of countries (particularly in the Commonwealth) that there would be no sporting ties between those countries and South Africa.

197 **Bob Geldoff.** Singer who undertook the Band Aid project to aid the starving people of Ethiopia. He was knighted.

198 **Pace College** (Soweto). Opened in 1982 and was established to create and strengthen black representation in commerce and finance. It was founded by the American Chamber of Commerce in South Africa.

199 **Tutu, Desmond** (1931-). South African Archbishop of the Anglican Church and General Secretary of the South African Council of Churches. In 1984 he received the Nobel Prize for Peace.

200 **Kennedy, Teddy** (1932-). US senator who campaigned for the presidency in 1980. He visited South Africa in 1985 and was harshly riduculed and condemned by black South Africans.

201 **Haile Selassie** (1891-1975). Emperor of Ethiopia from 1930. Before coming to the throne he was known as Ras Tafari. Despite his attempts at social and economic reform, his country remained one of the most backward in Africa and he was deposed in 1974.

202 **Haile Mariam Mengistu.** Took over from General Teferi Benti, who took over as Head of State of the Military Administration Council (Durg). Benti was killed in a gun battle between two factions of the Durg.

203 **Mohammed Reza Shah.** Son of Reza Pahlavi, who he succeeded to the throne to be the Shah of Iran. The Ayatollah Khomeni demanded the Shah's abdication in 1978, and in 1979 the Shah left Iran and died in Egypt in 1980.

204 **Khomeini, Rohallah** (1900-). Iranian Ayatollah and political leader. A Shi-ite Moslem he opposed attempts to westernize and secularize Iran. He became virtual head of state with the support of his Islamic Revoluation Party.

205 **Carter, Jimmy.** Thirty-ninth President of the US. He graduated from the US Naval

Academy in Annapolis (1946) and served as a electronics instructor. In 1953 he left the navy and returned home to manage the family peanut business. In July 1976 he won the Democratic presidential nomination and was elected president in November.

206 **World Council of Churches.** A union of Christian Churches from all over the world, engaged in extending Christian mission and unity throughout the world. It was founded in 1948.

207 **Kinnock, Neil Gordon** (1942-). British Labour Politician.

208 **Thatcher, Margaret Hilda** (1925-). British Conservative Politician who in February 1974 was elected leader of the Conservative Party and became Britain's first woman Prime Minister.

209 **Robespierre, Maximilien Francois Marie Isidore De** (1758-1794). French revolutionary leader, born at Arras. He was a leading lawyer, judge and litterateur in Arras until elected (1789) to the Estates-General, soon renamed the National Assembly.

210 **Gandhi, Mohandas Karamchand** (1869-1948). Indian religious and political leader known as Mahatma. Born in Porbander, in Kathiawar where his father had been chief minister. In 1913 he negotiated an agreement with J C Smuts raising the status of Indian labourers in South Africa. He was assassinated by a Hindu fanatic, N V Godso. Gandhi was one of the most influential and impressive figures of the 20th century.

211 **Hussein Saddam.** (1935-). King of Jordan from 1952. He is the great-grandson of King Hussein of the Hejaz. He succeeded his father, Talil to the Jordan throne. As a king he showed dexterity in maintaining himself in the Egyptian, and Israeli frontier incidents on his borders and also dealt with his own arab extremists.

212 **South African Council of Churches.** An ecumenical organisation comprised of the main line South African churches, which include the Anglican Church, Methodist Church, Presbyterian Church. The Council is affiliated to the World Council of Churches, although it is not a member.

213 **Jaap Marais.** The leader of the Herstigte Nasionale Party (HNP) a conservative political organization.

214 **Eugene Terre-Blanche.** Leader of the Afrikaner Weerstandsbeweging.

215 **Stormvolke.** Storm trooper.

216 **Troglodyte.** Cave dweller or cave man.

Index

Index

Credo Vusamazulu Mutwa

Credo Vusamazulu Mutwa was born on July 21, 1921, at a place called Umsinga Ferry in southern Natal, South Africa. In 1963 he was proclaimed a sanusi by his mother's family. He was later proclaimed High Sanusi and also Guardian of Tribal History and Tribal relics. Mutwa is a direct descendant of an unbroken line of Zulu High Witchdoctors and his great grandfather was the High Witchdoctor to the Zulu King, Dingane.

Today he lives in Mafikeng, Bophuthatswana, where he is working for the Bophuthatswana Government, building a traditional museum village.

Mutwa is the spiritual leader of the sanusis, inyangas and sangomas throughout the subcontinent (see notes) and as such is recognized as the spiritual leader of millions of black people. There are many black people who refer to him as "our priest and guardian of our culture." He is also regularly consulted as a traditional healer.

Despite his position as High Witchdoctor, Mutwa is known for his attempts to promote peace and reconciliation in South Africa. In the 1970s he built a traditional museum village in Soweto, the objective of which was to bring the black man closer to his roots and culture.

His peace efforts were met with bitter opposition and in 1976 he was forced to leave Soweto when his home was razed to the ground by radicals. He was directly involved in the Soweto riots of 1976 and attempted, in vain, to keep children away from the chaos and destruction. After spending some time in Natal he returned to Soweto only to live a life of fear and threats from political activists, and in December 1985 he again left Soweto and moved to Bophuthatswana.

Mutwa has also travelled extensively and has been involved in research projects in culture and religion. As a result of his writing and prophecies he has often been titled the "Homer of Africa."

Mutwa is perhaps best known for the two books he wrote on African tribal history, tribal customs and tribal religion — *Indaba My Children* and *Africa Is My Witness*. Published in the 1960s, both books became bestsellers and were published in a number of languages and countries. *Indaba My Children* is still being published to this day. Both books were an attempt to promote understanding between white and black.

This third book is another attempt to promote peace in South Africa . . . in what has been for Mutwa a life-long commitment.